# Asking
# the Right
# Questions

Seventh Edition

# Asking the Right Questions

## A Guide to Critical Thinking

M. Neil Browne

Stuart M. Keeley

*Bowling Green State University*

PEARSON

Prentice Hall

Upper Saddle River, New Jersey 07458

*Library of Congress Cataloging-in-Publication Data*

Browne, M. Neil, (date)
    Asking the right questions: a guide to critical thinking / M. Neil Browne, Stuart M.
    Keeley.—7th ed.
        p.      cm.
    Includes index.
    ISBN 0-13-182993-9
    1. Criticism.    2. Critical thinking.    I. Keeley, Stuart M., 1941-    II. Title.
    PN83.B785 2003
    808—dc21

                                                                                    2002044548

Editor-in-Chief: Leah Jewell
Senior Acquisitions Editor: Corey Good
Editorial Assistant: Steve Kyritz
Editorial/Production Supervision: Brittney Corrigan-McElroy
Prepress and Manufacturing Buyer: Mary Ann Gloriande
Cover Designer: Bruce Kenselaar
Cover Photograph: C McIntyre/Getty Images
Executive Marketing Manager: Brandy Dawson
Marketing Assistant: Christine Moodie

This book was set in 10/12 New Baskerville by Interactive Composition Corporation and was
printed by Maple Vail Book Mfg Group. The cover was printed by Coral Graphics Services.

About the cover: At first glance, you may have thought you were looking at a photograph of a
road sign somewhere in Europe. Did you question this initial impression? What did you first
notice about the sign? Did your mind start to realize that your initial assumption was wrong?
Why? This road sign is actually located in southern Maine, where many towns were given
European place names. In becoming a critical thinker, you learn to take control of your own
thought processes and go beyond the obvious by questioning, analyzing, and evaluating your
own thoughts and ideas.

 © 2004, 2001, 1998, 1994 by Pearson Education, Inc.
Upper Saddle River, New Jersey 07458

Printed in the United States of America

10  9  8  7  6  5  4  3  2

ISBN 0-13-182993-9

Pearson Education LTD., London
Pearson Education Australia PTY, Limited, Sydney
Pearson Education Singapore, Pte. Ltd
Pearson Education North Asia Ltd, Hong Kong
Pearson Education Canada, Ltd., Toronto
Pearson Educación de Mexico, S.A. de C.V.
Pearson Education—Japan, Tokyo
Pearson Education Malaysia, Pte. Ltd
Pearson Education, Upper Saddle River, New Jersey

# Contents

*109880*

## 11    Are the Statistics Deceptive?    155

## 12    What Significant Information Is Omitted?    165

## 13    What Reasonable Conclusions Are Possible?    179

# Preface

As a book ages, it becomes less and less the product of its original authors. The success of *Asking the Right Questions: A Guide to Critical Thinking* is a tribute to the sound advice we have received from the many readers who thought we could do better next time around and who told us so. In fact, one of our biggest challenges has been to pick and choose from among the suggestions.

Always uppermost in our mind has been the desire to retain the primary attributes of *Asking the Right Questions,* while adjusting to new emphases in our own thought and the evolving needs of our readers. For instance, while we can always think of dozens of additions that would, we believe, enhance new editions of *Asking the Right Questions,* we want most of all to keep the book readable and short. We are willing to pay the price of omitting several things that would be apposite in a more weighty treatment of critical thinking because those who adopt or learn from *Asking the Right Questions* have noted the crispness and cohesion of our approach so frequently. Individual readers who do not see their suggestions included will surely understand that writing for a general audience requires us to omit many valuable components that we would certainly include were we writing for a more specialized group of readers.

This new edition, like its predecessors, has been modified while retaining the basic framework of a simplified guide to critical thinking. Several new practice passages have been inserted. In addition, we have completely rewritten the fallacies chapter to make it more coherent and to provide new illustrations. But what is particularly fresh about the seventh edition are three new foci:

1. Emphasizing the positive dimensions of critical thinking so that users will be more eager to use the skills and attitudes they are learning;

2. Reminding readers frequently that each skill is but one part of a critical and constructive process that should culminate in tentative commitment; and

3. Creating a Web site containing multiple, diverse practice opportunities.

Learning critical thinking is neither simple nor easy. But even after critical thinking has been learned to some degree, there is still the challenge of desiring to use a process that can often be seen as rude, mean, or arrogant. None of us wishes to exhibit habits of mind that brand us as obnoxious. Yet at the same time, we do not want to base our behavior solely on the reactions of others to it; otherwise, we would just be a puppet of the crowd.

So we need to frame critical thinking in a manner that emphasizes its role in assisting us to make decisions that are both more reflective and caring as well. We learn critical thinking to be helpful to ourselves and to others. Critical thinking prevents us from courses of action that are inconsistent with whom we want to become. In addition, it assists others who are seeking beliefs and commitments built on relatively sound structures of reasoning. In those regards, critical thinking can be an act of friendship, moving others toward more reasonable beliefs and actions. The seventh edition tries to make that point in several contexts.

The second new focus in this edition is based on the fear that learning individual steps in any process can prevent our appreciation of the power of the entire process wherein all the steps are used in tandem. *Asking the Right Questions* builds the critical-thinking process one step at a time; each chapter introduces a particular critical-thinking skill. Subsequent chapters then add to the list of accumulating critical-thinking skills. But the entire rationale for learning the steps of critical thinking is to get ready to use them as a package, a cohesive assemblage of complementary abilities. Using the entire process of critical thinking is the most rewarding pathway to finding better arguments.

Finally, one thing that our readers request again and again are more practice materials. We are working with Prentice Hall to respond to that request with this new edition. The Web site for *Asking the Right Questions* will be organized by chapter and contain practice passages of varying size. In addition, learners also need to see arguments that are relatively strong. Critical thinking can move someone toward cynicism as she or he learns more about the multiple problems that can haunt daily reasoning. Hence, the Web site contains a lengthy, relatively strong argument concerning the efficacy of student evaluations of teaching. We want to highlight on the site what is particularly strong about this argument, to provide readers a model of what is possible when someone tries to reason well.

In addition, we wanted to provide on the Web site an illustration of critical analysis that is more realistic than the one provided in the final chapter. While agreeing with the appropriateness of the final chapter as a culmination of the algorithmic process of asking the right questions, several readers have urged us to provide a more realistic illustration. As they correctly point out, it is highly unrealistic to expect to see what is modeled in Chapter 14. We agree.

These new directions of *Asking the Right Questions* are meant to improve what our readers have told us they most want, a book that helps students toward reasonable autonomy. The success of previous editions of this book is potent testimony to our collective curiosity about what to believe. Our minds are under assault by experts and scam artists alike. Sorting among all their claims about what to eat, do, and believe is an incredibly difficult responsibility. We know that we need all the help we can get to protect ourselves from the dangers implicit in nonsense. We want to think carefully before we make a belief our own.

From the start of this book's history, we have been motivated by a variety of personal experiences and observations. First, we have been dismayed by the degree to which students and citizens in general increasingly depend on "experts," textbook writers, teachers, lawyers, politicians, journalists, and TV commentators. As the complexity of the world seems to increase at an accelerating rate, there is a greater tendency to become passive absorbers of information, uncritically accepting what is seen and heard. We are concerned that too many of us are not actively making personal choices about what to accept and what to reject.

Thus, the need for such a book is now even more pronounced. The use of "sound bites," the popularity of simplistic arguments, and the amount of information to which we are exposed every day have all increased dramatically. To encourage us all to use critical thinking more frequently as an antidote to this "information explosion" is our dream for *Asking the Right Questions.*

Our experience in teaching critical-thinking skills to our students over a number of years has convinced us that when individuals with diverse abilities are taught these skills in a simplified format, they can learn to apply them successfully. In the process, they develop greater confidence in their ability to make rational choices about social issues, even those with which they have formerly had little experience.

Thus, we have written a text that does a number of things that other books have failed to do. This text develops an integrated series of question-asking skills that can be applied widely. These skills are discussed in an informal style. (We have written to a general audience, not to any specialized group.)

The development of *Asking the Right Questions* has leaned heavily on our joint experience of 60 years as teachers of critical thinking. Our ideas have evolved in response to numerous classroom experiences with students at many different levels, from freshman to Ph.D. students.

These experiences have taught us certain emphases that are particularly effective in learning critical thinking. For instance, we provide many opportunities for the readers to apply their skills and to receive immediate feedback following the practice application. The book is replete with examples of writing devoted to controversial contemporary topics. The breadth of topics introduces the average reader to numerous controversies with which he or she may have little familiarity. The book is coherently organized, in that critical questions are discussed sequentially as the reader progresses from understanding to evaluating. In addition, it integrates cognitive and value dimensions—a very important aspect of critical thinking and personal decision making.

One feature that deserves to be highlighted is the applicability of *Asking the Right Questions* to numerous life experiences extending far beyond the classroom. The habits and attitudes associated with critical thinking are transferable to consumer, medical, legal, and general ethical choices. When our surgeon says surgery is needed, it can be life sustaining to seek answers to critical questions.

Who would find *Asking the Right Questions* especially beneficial? Because of our teaching experiences with readers representing many different levels of ability, we have difficulty envisioning any academic course or program for which this book would not be useful. In fact, the first five editions have been used in law, English, pharmacy, philosophy, education, psychology, sociology, religion, and social science courses, as well as in numerous high school classrooms.

A few uses for the book seem especially appropriate. Teachers in general education programs may want to begin their courses by assigning it as a coherent response to their students' requests to explain what is expected of them. English courses that emphasize expository writing could use this text both as a format for evaluating arguments prior to constructing an essay and as a checklist of problems that the writer should attempt to avoid as he or she writes. The book is especially functional in courses for training prospective teachers and graduate assistants because it makes explicit much that teachers will want to encourage in their students. Supplementing their current content with our step-by-step description of the process of critical reading and thinking may enrich courses in study-skill development. The text can also be used as the central focus of courses designed specifically to teach critical-reading and -thinking skills.

While *Asking the Right Questions* stems primarily from our classroom experiences, it is written so that it can guide the reading and listening habits of almost everyone. The skills that it seeks to develop are those that any critical reader needs in order for reading to serve as a basis for rational decisions.

The critical questions stressed in the book can enhance anyone's reasoning, regardless of the extent of his or her formal education.

This seventh edition owes special debts to many people. We wish to acknowledge the valuable advice of the following Prentice Hall reviewers: Brian Allan Wooters, Metropolitan Community College; JoAnn Carter-Wells, California State University at Fullerton; Jack R. Simmons, Savannah State University; Lisa Barnes, Delaware County Community College; Theresa Sullo, Albuquerque TVI Community College; David Critchett, Community College of Rhode Island; and Paul R. Frommer, University of Southern California, Marshall School of Business.

While our students are always a major source of suggested improvements, a few distinguished themselves in that regard. The seventh edition benefited from the valuable assistance of Emily Coplin, Allison Balcetis, and Jacob Castillo.

M. Neil Browne
Stuart M. Keeley

# THE BENEFIT OF ASKING
# THE RIGHT QUESTIONS

## Introduction

President Warren Harding often wondered aloud:

*What can I do?*

*I listen to one expert who tells me to do one thing.*

*Then I listen to another who tells me to do something else.*

*What can I do?*

All of us have been in President Harding's shoes before. What should we do? One possibility is to just agree with whatever we hear or read, and follow the advice of the person we last heard. But that approach gets us into deep trouble.

Consider the story of the newly elected judge to appreciate how dangerous that approach would be:

After listening to the opening statement of the prosecutor, the judge announced for all to hear, "you're right." The clerk gently reminded the judge that judges must wait until hearing the other side before deciding the case. Then after listening to the opening statement of the defense attorney, the judge announced excitedly, "you're correct." The clerk again explained that fairness required the judge to wait for the complete trial before announcing the verdict. The judge responded, "you're right."

The judge was certainly agreeable, but his task, like our lives, requires sorting out relative sense from nonsense. That sorting process is the project for this book.

We are bombarded with information. Every day we encounter new facts and opinions. In textbooks, newspapers, magazines, and on the Internet, writers present ideas they want us to accept.

In all areas of knowledge there are some issues where expert opinion is divided. You have the tough job of deciding which authority to believe. Whether you are reading a nursing journal, a critique of a poem, a textbook, or even the sports page, you will be faced with the problem of deciding which conclusions to accept, which to reject, and which to study further before committing to a decision.

As a thoughtful person you must make a choice about how you will react to what you see and hear. One alternative is to just accept whatever you encounter, as the new judge did in the story above; doing so automatically results in your making someone else's opinion your own. A more active alternative consists of asking questions in an effort to reach a personal decision about the worth of what you have experienced. This book is written for those who prefer the second alternative.

## Critical Thinking to the Rescue

Listening and reading critically—that is, reacting with systematic evaluation to what you have heard and read—requires a set of skills and attitudes. These skills and attitudes are built around a series of related critical questions. While we will learn them one by one, our goal is to be able to use them together to identify the best decision available.

We could have expressed them as a list of things you should do, but a system of questions is more consistent with the spirit of curiosity, wonder, and intellectual adventure essential to critical thinking. Thinking carefully is always an unfinished project; a story looking for an ending that will never arrive. Critical questions provide a stimulus and direction for critical thinking; they move us forward toward a continual, ongoing search for better opinions, decisions, or judgments.

Consequently, **critical thinking,** as we will use the term, refers to the following:

1. awareness of a set of interrelated critical questions,
2. ability to ask and answer critical questions at appropriate times, and the
3. desire to actively use the critical questions.

The goal of this book is to encourage you in all three of these dimensions.

Questions require the person being asked the question to act in response. By our questions, we are saying to the person: I am curious; I want to know more; help me. This request shows respect for the other person. The questions exist to inform and provide direction for all who hear them. In that respect critical thinking begins with the desire to improve what we think. The point of your questions is that you need help to have a deeper understanding or appreciation of what is being said.

The critical questions will be shared with you bit by bit, one question at a time. As a package, they will be useful whenever you choose to react to what you are hearing or reading. They are also useful in improving your own writing and speaking because they will assist you when you:

1. react critically to an essay or to evidence presented in a textbook, a periodical, or on a Web site,

2. judge the quality of a lecture or speech,

3. form an argument,

4. write an essay based on a reading assignment, or

5. participate in class.

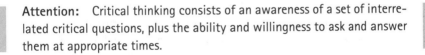

**Attention:**   Critical thinking consists of an awareness of a set of interrelated critical questions, plus the ability and willingness to ask and answer them at appropriate times.

As a citizen, you should find them especially helpful in shaping your voting behavior and your purchasing decisions, as well as improving your self-confidence by increasing your sense of intellectual independence.

## The Sponge and Panning for Gold: Alternative Thinking Styles

One approach to thinking is similar to the way in which a sponge reacts to water: by absorbing. This commonly used approach has some clear advantages.

First, the more information you absorb about the world, the more capable you are of understanding its complexities. Knowledge you have acquired provides a foundation for more complicated thinking later.

A second advantage of the sponge approach is that it is relatively passive. Rather than requiring strenuous mental effort, it tends to be rather quick and easy, especially when the material is presented in a clear and interesting fashion. The primary mental effort involves concentration and memory.

While absorbing information provides a productive start toward becoming a thoughtful person, the sponge approach has a serious disadvantage: It provides no method for deciding which information and opinions to believe and which to reject. If a reader relied on the sponge approach all the time, she would believe whatever she read last. The idea of being the mental puppet of whomever one happens to encounter is horrible imagery for a person and a community. Decisions become accidents of association, instead of reflective judgments.

We think you would rather choose for yourself what to absorb and what to ignore. To make this choice, you must read with a special attitude—a question-asking attitude. Such a thinking style requires active participation. The writer is trying to speak to you, and you should try to talk back to him, even though he is not present.

We call this interactive approach the panning-for-gold style of thinking. The process of panning for gold provides a model for active readers and listeners as they try to determine the worth of what they read and hear. The task is challenging and sometimes tedious, but the reward can be tremendous. To distinguish the gold from the gravel in a conversation requires you to ask frequent questions and to reflect on the answers.

The sponge approach emphasizes knowledge acquisition; the panning-for-gold approach stresses active interaction with knowledge as it is being acquired. Thus, the two approaches complement each other. To pan for intellectual gold, there must be something in your pan to evaluate. To evaluate arguments we must possess knowledge.

Let us examine more closely how the two approaches lead to different behavior. What does the individual who takes the sponge approach do when he reads material? He reads sentences carefully, trying to remember as much as he can. He may underline or highlight key words and sentences. He may take notes summarizing the major topics and major points. He checks his underlining or notes to be sure that he is not forgetting anything important. His mission is to find and understand what the author has to say. He memorizes the reasoning, but doesn't evaluate it.

What does the reader who takes the panning-for-gold approach do? Like the person using the sponge approach, he approaches his reading with the hope that he will acquire new knowledge. There the similarity ends. The panning-for-gold approach requires that the reader ask himself a number of questions designed to uncover the best available decisions or beliefs.

The reader who uses the panning-for-gold approach frequently questions why the author makes various claims. He writes notes to himself in the margins indicating problems with the reasoning. He continually interacts with the material. His intent is to critically evaluate the material and formulate personal conclusions based on the evaluation.

---

**Exhibit 1.1    MENTAL CHECK: *Am I Panning for Gold?***

√   Did I ask "why" someone wants me to believe something?

√   Did I take notes as I thought about potential problems with what was being said?

√   Did I evaluate what was being said?

√   Did I form my own conclusion about the topic?

---

## An Example of the Panning-for-Gold Approach

A major enduring issue in American society concerns what kind of gun control laws we need. Let's look at one position on this issue. Try to decide whether the argument is convincing.

> Arguments for banning guns are mostly myths, and what we need now is not more laws, but more law enforcement. One myth is that most murderers are ordinary, law-abiding citizens who kill a relative or acquaintance in a moment of anger only because a gun is available. In fact, every study of homicide shows the overwhelming majority of murderers are career criminals, people with lifelong histories of violence. The typical murderer has a prior criminal history averaging at least six years, with four major felony arrests.
>
> Another myth is that gun owners are ignorant rednecks given to senseless violence. However, studies consistently show that, on the average, gun owners are better educated and have more prestigious jobs than non-owners. To judge by their applications for permits to carry guns at all times, the following are (or were) gun owners: Eleanor Roosevelt, Joan Rivers, Donald Trump, and David Rockefeller.
>
> A further myth is that guns are not useful for self-defense. On the contrary! Every study has shown that handguns are used more often in repelling crimes than in committing them. While handguns are used in about 581,000 crimes yearly, they are used to repel about 645,000 crimes.

Even if gun laws do potentially reduce gun-related crime, the present laws are all that are needed if they are enforced. What good would stronger laws do when the courts have demonstrated that they will not enforce them?

If you apply the sponge approach to the passage, you probably will try to remember the reasons that we don't need further controls on guns. If so, you will have absorbed some knowledge. However, how convinced should you be by the reasons just mentioned? You can't evaluate them until you have applied the panning-for-gold approach to the passage—that is, until you have asked the right questions.

By asking the right questions, you would discover a number of possible weaknesses in the communicator's arguments. For instance, you might be concerned about all of the following:

1. What does the author mean by "overwhelming majority" or by "typical murderer"? Is the minority still a substantial number of murderers who kill relatives in a moment of anger?

2. What does "gun owners" mean? Are they the ones who buy the kinds of guns that gun control advocates are trying to ban?

3. How adequate were the cited research studies? Were the samples sufficiently large, random, and diverse?

4. Has the author lied with statistics by impressing us with large, rather precise numbers, like 581,000 and 645,000? What is the basis for these numbers? Can we rely on them?

5. What possible benefits of gun control are not mentioned? Have important studies that disagree with the author's position been omitted?

6. Is it legitimate to assume that because some famous people own guns that owning guns, then, is desirable? Do these people have special expertise concerning the pros and cons of gun ownership?

7. How many people are killed each year by handguns who would not have been killed were such guns not available?

8. Why did the person writing the essay fail to explain how we could encourage better enforcement of existing gun control laws to demonstrate his sensitivity to the harm that guns sometimes facilitate?

If you would enjoy asking these kinds of questions, this book is especially for you. Its primary purpose is to help you know when and how to ask questions that will enable you to decide what to believe.

The most important characteristic of the panning-for-gold approach is interactive involvement—a dialogue between the writer and the reader, or the speaker and the listener.

Clearly, there are times when the sponge approach is appropriate. Most of you have used it regularly and have acquired some level of success with it. It is much less likely that you are in the habit of employing the panning-for-gold approach—in part, simply because you have not had the appropriate training and practice. This book will not only help you ask the right questions, but will also provide frequent opportunities for practicing their use.

## Panning for Gold: Asking Critical Questions

It would be nice if what other people were really saying were always obvious, if all their essential thoughts were clearly labeled for us, if the writer or speaker never made an error in his or her reasoning, and if all knowledgeable people agreed about answers to important questions. If this were the case, we could read and listen passively and let others do our thinking for us.

However, the true state of affairs is quite the opposite. A person's reasoning is often not obvious. Important elements are often missing. Many of the elements that are present are unclear. Consequently, you need critical reading and listening skills to help you determine what makes sense and distinguish this clear thinking from the sloppy thinking that characterizes much of what you will encounter.

The inadequacies in what someone says will not always leap out at you. You must be an *active* searcher. You can do this by *asking questions*. The best search strategy is a critical-questioning strategy. A powerful advantage of these questions is that they permit you to ask searching questions even when you know very little about the topic being discussed. For example, you do not need to be an expert on childcare to ask critical questions about the adequacy of day-care centers.

## The Myth of the "Right Answer"

Our ability to find definite answers to questions often depends on the type of question that puzzles us. Scientific questions about the physical world are the most likely to have answers that reasonable people will accept, because the physical world is in certain ways more dependable or predictable than the social world. While the precise distance to the moon or the age of a newly discovered bone from an ancient civilization may not be absolutely certain, agreement about the dimensions of our physical environment is widespread. Thus, in the physical sciences, we frequently can arrive at "the right answer."

Questions about human behavior are different. The causes of human behavior are so complex that we frequently cannot do much more than form intelligent guesses about why or when certain behavior will occur. In addition, because many of us care a great deal about explanations and descriptions of human behavior, we prefer that explanations or descriptions of the rate of abortion, the frequency of unemployment, or the causes of child abuse be consistent with what we want to believe. Hence we bring our preferences to any discussion of those issues and resist arguments that are inconsistent with them.

Because human behavior is so controversial and complex, the best answers that we can find for many questions about our behavior will be probabilistic in nature. Even if we were aware of every bit of evidence about the effects of exercise on our mental health, we could still not expect certainty about those effects.

Regardless of the type of questions being asked, the issues that require your closest scrutiny are usually those about which "reasonable people" disagree. In fact, many issues are interesting exactly because there is strong disagreement about how to resolve them. Any controversy involves more than one position. Several positions may be supported with good reasons. There will seldom be a position on a social controversy about which you will be able to say, "This is clearly the right position on the issue." If such certainty were possible, reasonable people would not be debating the issue. Our focus in this book will be on such social controversies.

Even though you will not necessarily arrive at the "right answer" to social controversies, this book is designed to give you the skills to develop your best and most reasonable answer, given the nature of the problem and the available information. Decisions usually must be made in the face of uncertainty. Often we will not have the time or the ability to discover many of the important facts about a decision we must make. For example, it is simply unwise to ask all the right questions when someone you love is complaining of sharp chest pains and wants you to transport him to the emergency room.

## Thinking and Feeling

When you first encounter a conclusion, you do so with a history. You have learned to care about certain things, to support particular interests, and to discount claims of a particular type. So you always start to think critically in the midst of existing opinions. You have emotional commitments to these existing opinions. They are *your* opinions, and you quite understandably feel protective of them.

**This point deserves special emphasis. We bring lots of personal baggage to every decision we make—experiences, dreams, values, training, and cultural habits.**

However, if you are to grow, you need to recognize these feelings, and, as much as you are able, put them on a shelf for a bit. Only that effort will enable you to listen carefully when others offer arguments that threaten or violate your current beliefs. This openness is important because many of our own positions on issues are not especially reasonable ones; they are opinions given to us by others, and over many years we develop emotional attachments to them. Indeed, we frequently believe that we are being personally attacked when someone presents a conclusion contrary to our own. The danger of being emotionally involved in an issue is that you may fail to consider potential good reasons for other positions—reasons that might be sufficient to change your mind on the issue if only you would listen to them.

*Remember:* Emotional involvement should not be the primary basis for accepting or rejecting a position. Ideally, emotional involvement should be most intense *after* reasoning has occurred. Thus, when you read, try to avoid letting emotional involvement cut you off from the reasoning of those with whom you initially disagree. A successful active learner is one who is willing to change his or her mind. If you are ever to change your mind, you must be as open as possible to ideas that strike you as weird or dangerous when you first encounter them.

Critical thinkers, however, are not machines. They care greatly about many issues. The depth of that concern can be seen in their willingness to do all the hard mental work associated with critical thinking. But any passion felt by critical thinkers is moderated by the recognition that their current beliefs are open to revision.

## The Efficiency of Asking the Question, "Who Cares?"

Asking good questions is difficult but rewarding work. Some controversies will be much more important to you than others. When the consequences of a controversy for you and your community are minimal, you will want to spend less time and energy thinking critically about it than about more important controversies. For example, it makes sense to critically evaluate arguments for and against the protection of endangered species, because different positions on this issue lead to important consequences for society. It makes less sense to devote energy to evaluating whether blue is the favorite color of most corporate executives.

Your time is valuable. Before taking the time to critically evaluate an issue, ask the question, "Who cares?"

## Weak-Sense and Strong-Sense Critical Thinking

Previous sections mentioned that you already have opinions about many personal and social issues. You are willing right now to take a position on such questions as: Should prostitution be legalized? Is alcoholism a disease or willful misconduct? or, Was George Bush a successful president? You bring these initial opinions to what you hear and read.

Critical thinking can be used to either (1) defend *or* (2) evaluate and revise your initial beliefs. Professor Richard Paul's distinction between weak-sense and strong-sense critical thinking helps us appreciate these two antagonistic uses of critical thinking.

If you approach critical thinking as a method for defending your initial beliefs or those you are paid to have, you are engaged in *weak-sense critical thinking*. Why is it weak? To use critical-thinking skills in this manner is to be unconcerned with moving toward truth or virtue. The purpose of weak-sense critical thinking is to resist and annihilate opinions and reasoning different from yours. To see domination and victory over those who disagree with you as the objective of critical thinking is to ruin the potentially humane and progressive aspects of critical thinking.

In contrast, *strong-sense critical thinking* requires us to apply the critical questions to all claims, including our own. By forcing ourselves to look critically at our initial beliefs, we help protect against self-deception and conformity. It's easy to just stick with current beliefs, particularly when many people share them. But when we take this easy road, we run the strong risk of making mistakes we could otherwise avoid.

Strong-sense critical thinking does not necessarily force us to give up our initial beliefs. It can provide a basis for strengthening them because critical examination of those beliefs will sometimes reinforce our original commitment to them. A long time ago, John Stuart Mill warned us of the emptiness of a set of opinions accumulated without the help of strong-sense critical thinking:

> He who knows only his side of the case knows little of that. His reasons may have been good, and no one may have been able to refute them. But if he is equally unable to refute the reasons on the opposite side he has no ground for preferring either opinion.

To feel proud of a particular opinion it should be one we have selected—selected from alternative opinions that we have understood and evaluated.

## The Satisfaction of Using the Panning-for-Gold Approach

Doing is usually more fun than watching; doing well is more fun than simply doing. If you start using the interactive process taught in this book, you can feel the same sense of pride in your reading and listening that you normally get from successful participation in physical activities.

> **Attention:**  Weak-sense critical thinking is the use of critical thinking to defend your current beliefs. Strong-sense critical thinking is the use of the same skills to evaluate all claims and beliefs, especially your own.

Critical thinkers find it satisfying to know when to say "no" to an idea or opinion and to know why that response is appropriate. If you regularly use the panning-for-gold approach, then anything that gets into your head will have been systematically examined first. When an idea or belief *does* pass the criteria developed here, it will make sense to agree with it—at least until new evidence appears.

Imagine how good you will feel if you know *why* you should ignore or accept a particular bit of advice. Frequently, those faced with an opinion different from their own respond by saying, "Oh, that's just your opinion." But the issue should not be whose opinion it is, but rather whether it is a good opinion. Armed with the critical questions discussed in this book, you can experience the satisfaction of knowing why certain advice is nonsense.

The sponge approach is often satisfying because it permits you to accumulate information. Though this approach is productive, there is much more gratification in being a participant in a meaningful dialogue with the writer or speaker. Reading and listening become much richer as you begin to see things that others may have missed. As you learn to select information and opinions systematically, you will probably desire to read more and more in a lifelong effort to decide which advice makes sense.

## Trying Out New Answers

Although there is often no absolutely right answer, this book tries to encourage your search for better answers. Certainly, some answers are more accurate, appropriate, useful, or moral than are others. For you to want to do the hard work necessary to find better answers, you need substantial curiosity and even courage.

Courage is required because to keep looking for better answers, we have to be willing to give up our current beliefs or positions. When we encounter a question, we probably already have an answer. Suppose someone says something to us about the appropriateness of behavior by abortion activists. In all probability we already have an opinion about the matter.

We don't listen to someone's argument with a blank slate. We feel a sense of ownership about opinions we call our own. It often takes incredible courage to give up on an opinion we have held for some time after listening to someone else. As critical thinkers, we have to struggle to force ourselves to try out new answers. The interplay between our old answers and new ones provides a basis for our growth.

## Effective Communication and Critical Thinking

Many of the skills you will learn, as you become a more critical thinker will improve the quality of your writing and speaking. As you write and speak, it helps to be aware of the expectations careful thinkers will have. Because your objective is communication, many of the questions the thoughtful person will ask in evaluating your writing or speech should serve as guides for your own attempts to communicate well. Several of the critical questions that we urge you to ask highlight problems you will want to avoid as you write or speak.

While the emphasis in this book is on effective thinking, the link to competent communication is so direct that it will be a theme throughout. Wherever appropriate, we will mention how the skill being encouraged is an aid to improved communication.

## The Importance of Practice

Learning new critical-thinking skills is a lot like learning new physical skills. You cannot learn simply by being told what to do or by watching others. You have to practice, and frequently the practice will be both rewarding and hard work. Our goal is to make your learning as simple as possible. However, acquiring the habit of critical thinking will initially take a lot of practice.

The practice exercises and sample responses at the end of each chapter are an important part of this text. Try to do the exercises and, only then, compare your answers with ours. Our answers are not necessarily the only correct ones, but they provide illustrations of how to apply the question-asking skills. We intentionally failed to provide sample answers for the third passage at the end of each chapter. Our objective is to give you the opportunity to struggle with the answer using your knowledge of the chapter you have just studied. We want you to feel the accomplishment of no longer necessarily needing us to guide you.

## The Right Questions

To give you an initial sense of the skills that *Asking the Right Questions* will help you acquire, we will list the critical questions for you here. By the end of the book, you should know when and how to ask these questions productively:

1.  What are the issues and the conclusions?
2.  What are the reasons?
3.  Which words or phrases are ambiguous?
4.  What are the value conflicts and assumptions?
5.  What are the descriptive assumptions?
6.  Are there any fallacies in the reasoning?
7.  How good is the evidence?
8.  Are there rival causes?
9.  Are the statistics deceptive?
10. What significant information is omitted?
11. What reasonable conclusions are possible?

# WHAT ARE THE ISSUE AND THE CONCLUSION?

Before we evaluate someone's reasoning, we must first find it. Doing so sounds simple; it isn't. To get started as a critical thinker, you must practice the identification of the issue and the conclusion.

> Fraternities and sororities are often involved in charitable activities. They provide volunteers to raise money for many worthwhile causes. Their contribution in this regard deserves our praise.
>
> Yet we cannot stop our description of Greek organizations with this incomplete picture. Their good deeds are overwhelmed by their encouragement of conformity, childish pranks, and anti-intellectual antics. The abundant talents of their members should be channeled elsewhere.

The person who wrote this assessment of Greek organizations very much wants you to believe something. In general, those who create Web pages, editorials, books, magazine articles, or speeches are trying to alter your perceptions or beliefs. For you to form a reasonable reaction, you must first identify the controversy or *issue* as well as the thesis or conclusion being pushed onto you. (Someone's *conclusion* is his or her intended message to you. Its purpose is to shape your beliefs and/or behavior.) Otherwise, you will be reacting to a distorted version of the attempted communication.

When you have completed this chapter, you should be able to answer the first of our critical questions successfully:

[?]  *Critical Question:* **What are the issue and the conclusion?**

**Attention:**   An issue is a question or controversy responsible for the conversation or discussion. It is the stimulus for what is being said.

## Kinds of Issues

It will be helpful at this point to identify two kinds of issues you will typically encounter. The following questions illustrate one of these:

**Do** families who own pets have fewer arguments with one another?

**What** causes high blood pressure?

**Who** made the decision to increase our sales taxes?

**How** much will college cost in the year 2010?

All these questions have one thing in common. They demand answers that attempt to describe the way the world is, was, or is going to be. For example, answers to the first two questions might be, "In general, families with pets have fewer arguments with one another," and "Poor dietary habits cause high blood pressure."

Such issues are *descriptive issues*. They are commonly found in textbooks, magazines, the Internet, and television. Such issues reflect our curiosity about patterns or order in the world. Note the boldfaced words that begin each question above; when questions begin with these words, they will probably be descriptive questions.

**Attention:**   Descriptive issues are those that raise questions about the accuracy of descriptions of the past, present, or future.

Now let's look at examples of a second kind of question:

**Should** capital punishment be abolished?

**What ought to be done** about unemployment?

**Must** we outlaw SUVs or face increasing rates of asthma?

All of these questions demand answers that suggest the way the world *ought to be*. For example, answers to the first two questions might be, "Capital punishment *should be* abolished," and "We *ought* to reduce the unemployment rate."

These issues are ethical, or moral, issues; they raise questions about what is right or wrong, desirable or undesirable, good or bad. They demand prescriptive answers. Thus, we will refer to these issues as *prescriptive issues*. Social controversies are often prescriptive issues.

We have somewhat oversimplified. Sometimes it will be difficult to decide what kind of issue is being discussed. It will be useful to keep these distinctions in mind, however, because the kinds of critical evaluations you eventually make will differ depending on the kind of issue to which you are responding.

**Attention:**   Prescriptive issues are those that raise questions about what we should do or what is right or wrong, good or bad.

## Searching for the Issue

How does one go about determining the basic question or issue? Sometimes it is very simple: The writer or speaker will tell you what it is. Alternatively, the issue may be identified in the body of the text, usually right at the beginning, or it may even be found in the title. When the issue is explicitly stated, it will be indicated by phrases such as the following:

> *The question I am raising is:* Why must we have speed limits on our highways?
>
> Lowering the legal drinking age: *Is it the right thing to do?*
>
> *Should* sex education be taught in the school?

Unfortunately, the question is not always explicitly stated and instead must be inferred from other clues in the communication. For example, many writers or speakers are reacting to some current event that concerns them, such as a series of violent acts in schools. Asking "What is the author reacting to?" will often suggest the central issue of a communication. Another good clue is knowledge of the author's background, such as organizations to which he belongs. So check for background information about the author as you try to determine the issue.

When you are identifying the issue, try to resist the idea that there is one and only one correct way to state the issue. Once you have found a question that the entire essay or speech is addressing, and you can show the link between that question and the essay or speech, *you have found the issue.* Just make certain that what you are calling an issue meets the definitional criteria for that idea.

The surest way to detect an issue when it's not explicitly stated, however, is to locate the conclusion. In many cases the conclusion must be found before you can identify the issue. Thus, in such cases, the first step in critical evaluation is to find the conclusion—a frequently difficult step.

**We cannot critically evaluate until we find the conclusion!**

Let's see how we go about looking for that very important structural element.

**Attention:**   A conclusion is the message that the speaker or writer wishes you to accept.

## Searching for the Author's or Speaker's Conclusion

To identify the conclusion, the critical thinker must ask, "What is the writer or speaker trying to prove?" or "What is the communicator's main point?" The answer to either of these questions will be the conclusion. Any answer to the question provided by the speaker or writer will be the conclusion.

In searching for a conclusion, you will be looking for a statement or set of statements that the writer or speaker wants you to believe. She wants you to believe the conclusion on the basis of her other statements. In short, the basic structure of persuasive communication or argument is: *This* because of *that. This* refers to the conclusion; *that* refers to the support for the conclusion. This structure represents the process of *inference.*

Conclusions are *inferred;* they are derived from reasoning. Conclusions are ideas that require other ideas to support them. Thus, whenever someone claims something is true or ought to be done and provides no statements to support his claim, that claim is not a conclusion because no one has offered any basis for belief. In contrast, unsupported claims are what we refer to as *mere* opinions.

The last paragraph says a lot. It would be a good idea for you to read it again. Understanding the nature of a conclusion is an essential step toward critical reading and listening. Let's look closely at a conclusion and at the inference process. Here is a brief paragraph; see whether you can identify the conclusion, then the statements that support it.

We oppose building a nuclear waste facility in Nevada. We believe that there are safer ways to store the dangerous by-products of nuclear energy.

"We oppose building a nuclear waste facility in Nevada" is this writer's answer to the question of whether we should store nuclear waste in Nevada; it is her conclusion. She supports the conclusion (a belief) with another belief: "there are safer ways to store the dangerous by-products of nuclear energy."

Do you see why the later belief is not a conclusion? It is not the conclusion because it is used to prove something else. *Remember:* To believe one statement (the conclusion) because you think it is well supported by *other* beliefs is to make an inference. When people engage in this process, they are reasoning; the conclusion is the outcome of this reasoning.

Sometimes communicators will not make their conclusions explicit; in such cases you will have to infer the conclusion from what you believe the author is trying to prove by the set of ideas she has presented.

## USING THIS CRITICAL QUESTION

Once you have found the conclusion, use it as the focus of your evaluation. It is the destination that the writer or speaker wants you to choose. Your ongoing concern is: Should I accept that conclusion on the basis of what is supporting the claim?

## Clues to Discovery: How to Find the Conclusion

There are a number of clues to help you identify the conclusion.

CLUE NO. 1: **Ask what the issue is.** Because a conclusion is always a response to an issue, it will help you find the conclusion if you know the issue. We discussed earlier how to identify the issue. First, look at the title. Next, look at the opening paragraphs. If this technique doesn't help, skimming several pages may be necessary.

CLUE NO. 2: **Look for indicator words.** The conclusion will frequently be preceded by indicator words that announce a conclusion is coming. When you see these indicator words, take note of them. They tell you that a conclusion may follow. A list of such indicator words follows:

| | |
|---|---|
| consequently | suggests that |
| hence | it should be clear that |
| in fact | we may deduce that |
| therefore | points to the conclusion that |
| thus | the point I'm trying to make is |
| in short | the most obvious explanation |
| it follows that | it is highly probable that |
| shows that | proves that |
| indicates that | the truth of the matter is |

Read the following passage; then identify and highlight the indicator words. By doing so, you will have identified the statements containing the conclusion.

But now, more than two years after voters overwhelmingly approved the lottery, it has been proven that the game is not a success; in fact, it can be considered a failure.

First of all, during the campaign for passage of the lottery, the public was repeatedly told that the proceeds would go toward curing the financial ills of both higher education institutions and local primary and secondary schools. It was on this premise that the lottery received overwhelming support from the public. Not until it was approved, however, was it widely conceded that lottery profits would go into the general fund instead of the state's education budget. Less than half of the lottery's profits go to education.

You should have highlighted the following phrases: *it has been proven,* and *in fact.* The conclusions follow these words.

Unfortunately, many written and spoken communications do not introduce the conclusion with indicator words. However, when *you* write, you should draw attention to your thesis with indicator words. Those words act as a neon sign, drawing attention to the point you want the reader to accept.

CLUE NO. 3: **Look in likely locations.** Conclusions tend to occupy certain locations. The first two places to look are at the beginning and at the end.

Many writers begin with a statement of purpose, containing what they are trying to prove. Others summarize their conclusions at the end. If you are reading a long, complex passage and are having difficulty seeing where it is going, skip ahead to the end.

CLUE NO. 4: **Remember what a conclusion is not.** Conclusions will not be any of the following:

- examples
- statistics
- definitions
- background information
- evidence

CLUE NO. 5: **Check the context of the communication and the author's background.** Often writers, speakers, or Internet sites take predictable positions on issues. Knowing probable biases of the source and the background of authors can be especially valuable clues when the conclusion is not explicit. Be especially alert to information about organizations with which writers or speakers may be associated.

CLUE NO. 6: **Ask the question, "and therefore?"** Because conclusions are often implied, ask for the identity of the "and therefore" element. Ask, "Does the author want us to draw an implied conclusion from the information communicated?" Conclusions like "candidate X will be soft on crime" are often left for the reader or viewer to infer from the limited information presented in a political ad.

## Critical Thinking and Your Own Writing and Speaking

Because readers of your writing will be looking for *your* thesis or conclusion, help them by giving it the clarity it deserves. It is the central message you want to deliver. Emphasize it; leave no doubt about what it actually is. Making your conclusion easily identifiable not only makes a reader's task easier, it also may improve the logic of your writing. An effective way to emphasize the conclusion is to insert it at the beginning or end of your essay and precede it with an indicator word.

In addition, take a close look at your conclusion to make certain that it is a direct response to the issue you intended to address. For example, suppose the issue you are attempting to address is: Will owning a pet increase how long we live? If your conclusion is: "yes, it will increase our life span by an average of 15 years," there is a match between issue and conclusion. But were your conclusion, instead, that pets bring joy to the lives of everyone who owns them, your reasoning is confused. The latter conclusion is responding to a different issue, namely, do pets bring joy to our lives?

## Practice Exercises

 *Critical Question:* **What are the issue and the conclusion?**

In the following passages locate the issue and conclusion. As you search, be sure to look for indicator words.

### Passage 1

Day-care centers and babysitters are becoming more and more popular as greater numbers of women enter the workforce. Although mothers may enjoy working outside the home, they might be harming their children when they hand them over to someone else for care during work hours.

This current trend means that some women return to their workplace very soon after a child has been born. Although job requirements may prompt this hasty return to the workforce, women must reevaluate their priorities. Having a child is a major responsibility, and women must realize that children must come first.

Who can provide the love and attention that young children desperately need for their emotional and physical development? While a babysitter might feel affection for a child, only a mother could offer her child unconditional love and encouragement. Also, children do not get as much individual attention at day-care centers.

While a job might provide extra money for a household, mothers must realize that their children are more valuable than money. Therefore, mothers should stay at home with their children.

### Passage 2

When people consider the subject of false or repressed memories, many seem to discount hypnosis as a plausible procedure. The media has printed numerous stories of the false accusations made by people under hypnosis.

In fact, hypnosis is a credible method of treatment in a variety of areas. Hypnosis can be used for medical treatment as a method of relaxation. Hypnotized patients learn to focus their attention on particular aspects of their environment and ignore the rest. Furthermore, psychologists also use hypnosis to treat neurotic symptoms, phobias, and memory problems.

The existence of one negative use of hypnosis has clouded the beneficial aspects of the procedure. Although a few cases of false memories have arisen from the use of hypnosis, it is still often a useful treatment procedure.

### Passage 3

Studies suggest that setting aside time for recess for high-school-aged students makes them more alert; thus, they have higher grades.

Several high schools across the country have experimented with twenty-minute or thirty-minute blocks of free time for the students to either exercise or spend time with friends. This time permits students to relax and not get burned out on thinking for seven hours a day.

Researchers noticed that classes taken later in the day at these schools had a higher-than-normal number of students with grades of A's and B's. It seems clear that recess is a helpful tool for students to be more academically successful in school.

## Sample Responses

### Passage 1

Because the author of the passage does not explicitly state a question, or issue, we must infer it by her conclusion and the concerns she raises throughout the passage. The first three paragraphs all mention problems that arise when mothers work outside the home. Both the indicator *therefore* and the location suggest that the final sentence of the fourth paragraph is the author's conclusion. Notice that this final sentence provides an answer to the issue just as a conclusion should do. Notice also that this is a prescriptive issue; it asks: What ought to be done?

ISSUE: *Should mothers work outside the home?*

CONCLUSION: *Mothers should forgo work outside the home to care for their children.*

### Passage 2

The first paragraph establishes the issue. It tells us what is on the writer's mind. The second sets the record straight from the perspective of the writer. The words *in fact* let you know that a conclusion is on the way. The third paragraph then indicates the rarity of the abuse of hypnosis. The point is that the negative effects of hypnosis are rare compared to the positive effects.

Notice that this issue has both prescriptive and descriptive features. Depending on whether we interpret the author's intent as a prescription that hypnosis should be used, or as a description of the effects of hypnosis. We believe that when someone touts the benefits of a procedure (or movie, restaurant, or candidate) that person is implying that certain actions *should* be taken. Thus, we stated the issue in prescriptive form.

ISSUE:  *Should hypnosis be considered a useful psychological tool?*

CONCLUSION:  *Yes, hypnosis is a beneficial procedure.*

## CRITICAL QUESTION SUMMARY: WHY THIS QUESTION IS IMPORTANT

### What Are the Issue and the Conclusion?

Before you can evaluate an author's argument, you must clearly identify the issue and conclusion. How can you evaluate an argument if you don't know exactly what the author is trying to persuade you to believe? Finding an author's main point is the first step in deciding whether you will accept or reject it.

# WHAT ARE THE REASONS?

Reasons provide answers for our human curiosity about why someone makes a particular decision or holds a particular opinion.

> Every class should conclude with student evaluations.

> A pig is smarter than a mule.

> Employers should be able to fire any employee who refuses to take a drug test.

Those three claims are each missing something. We may or may not agree with them, but in their current form they are neither weak nor strong. None of the claims contains an explanation or rationale for *why* we should agree. Thus, if we heard someone make one of those three assertions, we would be left hungry for more.

What is missing is the reason or reasons responsible for the claims. *Reasons* are beliefs, evidence, metaphors, analogies, and other statements offered to support or justify conclusions. They are the statements that together form the basis for demonstrating the credibility of a conclusion. Chapter 2 gave you some guidelines for locating two very important parts of the structure of an argument—the issue and the conclusion. This chapter focuses on techniques for identifying the third essential element of an argument—the reasons.

When a writer has a conclusion she wants you to accept, she must present reasons to persuade you that she is right, and to show you *why*.

It is the mark of a rational person to support his or her beliefs with adequate proof, especially when the beliefs are of a controversial nature. For example, when someone asserts that we should exclude inexperienced lawyers from representing those charged with felonies, this assertion should be met with the challenge, "Why do you say that?" You should raise this question whether you agree or disagree.

The person's reasons may be either strong or weak, but you will not know until you have asked the question and identified the reasons. If the answer is "because I think so," you should be dissatisfied with the argument, because the "reason" is a mere restatement of the conclusion. However, if the answer is evidence concerning serious mistakes made by inexperienced lawyers in felony cases, you will want to consider such evidence when you evaluate the conclusion. Remember: *You cannot determine the worth of a conclusion until you identify the reasons.*

Identifying reasons is a particularly important step in critical thinking. An opinion cannot be evaluated fairly unless we ask why it is held and get a satisfactory response. Focusing on reasons requires us to remain open to and tolerant of views that might differ from our own. If we reacted to conclusions rather than to reasoning, we would tend to stick to the conclusions we brought to the discussion or essay, and those conclusions that agree with our own would receive our rapid assent. If we are ever to reexamine our own opinions, we must stay open to the reasons provided by those people with opinions that we do not yet share.

 *Critical Question:* **What are the reasons?**

## Reasons + Conclusion = Argument

In ordinary conversation an argument refers to a disagreement, a time when blood pressure soars. We will use the concept in a very different manner. An *argument* is a combination of two forms of statements: a conclusion and the reasons allegedly supporting it. The partnership between reasons and conclusion establishes a person's argument. It is something we provide because we care about how people live their lives and what they believe. Our continual improvement depends on someone's caring enough about us to offer us arguments and to evaluate the ones we make.

Sometimes an argument will consist of a single reason and a conclusion; often, however, several reasons will be offered to support the conclusion. So when we refer to someone's argument, we might be referring to a single reason and its related conclusion or to the entire group of reasons and the conclusion it is intended to substantiate.

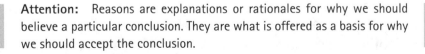

**Attention:**   Reasons are explanations or rationales for why we should believe a particular conclusion. They are what is offered as a basis for why we should accept the conclusion.

As we use the terms, *argument* and *reasoning* mean the same thing—the use of one or more ideas to support another idea. Thus when a communication lacks reasons, it is neither an argument nor an example of reasoning. Consequently, only arguments and reasoning can be logically flawed. Because a reason *by itself* is an isolated idea, it cannot reflect a logical relationship.

Several characteristics of arguments grab our attention:

- They have an intent. Those who provide them hope to convince us to believe certain things or act in certain ways. Consequently, they call for a reaction. We can imitate the sponge or the gold prospector, but we ordinarily must respond somehow.

- Their quality varies. Critical thinking is required to determine the extent of quality in an argument.

- They have two essential visible components—a conclusion and reasons. Failure to identify either component destroys the opportunity to evaluate the argument. We cannot evaluate what we cannot identify.

That last point deserves some repetition and explanation. There is little purpose in rushing critical thinking. Taking the time to locate arguments before we assess what we think was said is only fair to the person providing the argument.

## Initiating the Questioning Process

The first step in identifying reasons is to approach the argument with a questioning attitude, and the first question you should ask is a *why* question. You have identified the conclusion; now you wish to know why the conclusion makes sense. If a statement does not answer the question, "Why does the writer or speaker believe that?" then it is not a reason. To function as a reason, a statement (or group of statements) must provide support for a conclusion.

Let us apply the questioning attitude to the following paragraph. First we will find the conclusion; then we will ask the appropriate *why* question. Remember your guidelines for finding the conclusion. (The indicator words for the conclusion have been italicized.)

(1) Is the cost of hospital care outrageous? (2) A recent survey by the American Association of Retired Persons offers reliable evidence on this issue. (3) Independent audits of the bills of 2,000 patients found that hospitals overcharge their patients by an average of 15 percent. (4) In addition, exit interviews with

400 patients revealed high amounts of dismay and anger when the patients were informed about the size of their total hospital bill. (5) *In short,* the costs of hospital care are much too high.

What follows *In short* answers the question raised in statement (1). Thus, the conclusion is statement (5) ". . . the costs of hospital care are much too high." *Highlight the conclusion!*

 **Attention:**   An argument consists of a conclusion and the reasons that allegedly support it.

We then ask the question, "Why does the writer or speaker believe the conclusion?" The statements that answer that question are the reasons. In this particular case, the writer provides us with evidence as reasons. Statements (3) and (4) jointly provide the evidence; that is, together they provide support for the conclusion. Together they serve as the reason for the conclusion. Thus, we can paraphrase the reason as: A survey shows that hospitals overcharge their patients and that patients are greatly shocked by the size of their hospital bills.

Now, try to find the reasons in the following paragraph. Again, first find the conclusion, highlight it, and then ask the *why* question.

(1) Euthanasia is detrimental to the welfare of society because it destroys your ideas of sacrifice, loyalty, and courage in bearing pain. (2) Some dying persons accept their suffering as a way of paying for their sins. (3) These people should be permitted to die as they wish—without help from any other person in speeding up the dying process.

There is no obvious indicator word for the conclusion in the paragraph, but the author is clearly arguing against the morality of euthanasia. The conclusion here is: "Euthanasia is detrimental to the welfare of society." Why does the author believe this? The major reason given is that "it destroys your ideas of sacrifice, loyalty, and courage in bearing pain." The next two sentences in the excerpt provide additional support for this reason.

One of the best ways for you to determine whether you have discovered a reason is to try to play the role of the communicator. Put yourself in her position and ask yourself, "Why am I in favor of this conclusion that I am supporting?" Try to put into your own words how you believe the communicator would answer this question. If you can paraphrase the answer, you have probably discovered her reasons.

As you determine a communicator's reasoning structure, you should treat any idea that seems to be used to support his conclusion as a reason, even if you do not believe it provides support for the conclusion.

## Words That Identify Reasons

As was the case with conclusions, there are certain words that will typically indicate that a reason will follow. *Remember:* The structure of reasoning is *this, because of that.* Thus, the word *because,* as well as words synonymous with and similar in function to it, will frequently signal the presence of reasons. A list of indicator words for reasons follows:

| | |
|---|---|
| as a result of | for the reason that |
| because of the fact that | in view of |
| first, . . . second | is supported by |
| for | since the evidence is |
| for example | researchers found that |
| for one thing | |

## Kinds of Reasons

There are many different kinds of reasons, depending on the kind of issue. Many reasons will be statements that present evidence. By *evidence,* we mean specific information that someone uses to furnish "proof" for something she is trying to claim is true. Communicators appeal to many kinds of evidence to "prove their point." These include "the facts," research findings, examples from real life, statistics, appeals to experts and authorities, personal testimonials, metaphors, and analogies. Different kinds of evidence are more appropriate in some situations than in others, and you will find it helpful to develop rules for yourself for determining what kinds of evidence are appropriate on given occasions.

You will often want to ask, "What kind of evidence is needed to support this claim?" and then determine whether such evidence has been offered. You should know that there are no uniform "codes of evidence" applicable to all cases of serious reasoning. A more detailed treatment of evidence appears in Chapters 8–11.

When a speaker or writer is trying to support a descriptive conclusion, the answer to the *why* question will typically be evidence.

The following example provides a descriptive argument; try to find the author's reasons.

> (1) The fact is that college women are now smoking cigarettes at an increasing rate. (2) Recent surveys show that as male college students have decreased their consumption by 40 percent, females have increased their consumption of cigarettes by 60 percent.

You should have identified the first statement as the conclusion. It is a descriptive statement about the rate at which women in college are smoking cigarettes. The rest of the paragraph presents the evidence—the reason for the conclusion. *Remember:* The conclusion itself will not be evidence; it will be a belief supported by evidence or by other beliefs.

In prescriptive arguments, reasons are typically either general, prescriptive statements, or they are descriptive beliefs or principles. The use of these kinds of statements to support a conclusion in a prescriptive argument is illustrated in the following:

> (1) With regard to the big controversy over grade inflation, I would like to ask a few questions. (2) What difference does it make if the people who are really good are never distinguished from the average student? (3) Is there a caste system in our society according to grade-point averages?
>
> (4) Are those with high grade-point averages superior to those with low grade-point averages? (5) In the majority of cases, grades are not a true indication of learning, anyway; they are a measure of how well a student can absorb information for a short time period and regurgitate it on a test.
>
> (6) Students will retain the information that interests them and is important. (7) Why can't we eliminate grades and be motivated only by the inborn curiosity and zest for learning that is really in us all?

The controversy here is what to do about grade inflation. The author's solution to the problem is to abolish grades, as indicated in sentence (7). Let's look for sentences that answer the question, "Why does the author believe this conclusion?" First, note that no evidence is presented. Sentences (2) and (3) jointly form one reason: It is not important to distinguish the average student from the good student. Note that this is a general principle that indicates the writer's view about how the world should be. Sentences (4) and (5) add a second reason: Grades are not a true indicator of learning. This is a general belief regarding a disadvantage of grades. Sentence (6) provides a third reason: Students will retain only the information that interests them and is important (grades do not help learners to remember). This reason is another general belief. If the argument were expanded by the author, the beliefs themselves might be supported by evidence in some form.

## Keeping the Reasons and Conclusions Straight

Much reasoning is long and not very well organized. Sometimes a set of reasons will support one conclusion, and that conclusion will function as the main reason for another conclusion. Reasons may be supported by other reasons. In especially complicated arguments, it is frequently difficult to keep the structure straight in your mind as you attempt to critically evaluate what you have read. To overcome this problem, try to develop your own organizing procedure for keeping the reasons and conclusions separate and in a logical pattern.

---

### Clues for Identifying and Organizing the Reasoning of a Passage

1. Circle indicator words.

2. Underline the reasons and conclusion in different colors of ink, or highlight the conclusion and underline the reasons.

3. Label the reasons and conclusion in the margin.

4. After reading long passages, make a list of reasons at the end of the essay.

5. For especially complicated reasoning, diagram the structure, using numbers to refer to each reason and conclusion and arrows to designate the direction of their relationships. Sometimes this technique is most effective if all reasons and conclusions are first paraphrased in the margins, then numbered.

---

We can illustrate these suggested techniques by attempting to find the conclusion and reasons in the following relatively complex passage.

(1) Do physicians have a moral obligation to provide free medical care for those who cannot pay? (2) *Yes, they do.* (3) *First,* society has restricted most medical practice to physicians, resulting in a medical monopoly that has obvious benefits. (4) *Thus, it seems reasonable that* the profession acknowledge its collective responsibility to provide care even to those who cannot pay.

(5) *Second,* the moral obligation of individual physicians to provide free care derives from an understanding of their special role. (6) Physicians should not be compared to plumbers or car mechanics, or to other craftsmen who repair

inanimate objects. (7) Unlike automobile repairs, the health problems of people are not deferrable or negotiable. (8) That doctors help some people without pay is essential if doctors are to remain doctors and medical services are not to be regarded as just another form of profit-seeking business activity.

Initially you should notice that we have italicized the conclusion and key indicator words. As you read this passage, you surely noticed that the reasoning structure is quite complicated. For such a passage, we have to understand the logical sequence of sentences to isolate the reasoning structure. Thus we have diagrammed the relationships among the reasons and conclusion. Try to diagram this passage on your own; then, compare your diagram to ours.

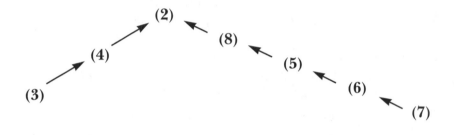

Our diagram reflects our interpretation that sentence (4) in paragraph 1 and sentence (8) in paragraph 2 directly answered the question, "Why is the conclusion, sentence (2), true?" The direction of the rest of the arrows in the diagram denotes how we believe these two reasons are supported by further reasons. For example, statement (6) provides support for (5).

Diagramming is useful for gaining an understanding of especially complicated arguments. When reading lengthy essays, it is always useful to paraphrase the main reasons in the margins. Thus, for the above passage, we might have supplied the following paraphrased reasons:

Paragraph 1: Physicians owe a debt to society.

Paragraph 2: The physician's role is special; physicians are unlike businessmen.

We have mentioned a number of techniques for you to use in developing a clear picture of the reasoning structure. If some other technique works better for you, by all means use it. The important point is to keep the reasons and conclusions straight as you prepare to evaluate.

## USING THIS CRITICAL QUESTION

Once you have found the reasons, you need to come back to them again and again as you read or listen further. Their quality is crucial to a strong argument. The conclusion depends on their merit. *Weak reasons create weak reasoning!*

## Reasons First, Then Conclusions

The first chapter warned you about the danger of weak-sense critical thinking. A warning signal that can alert you to weak-sense critical thinking should go off when you notice that reasons seem to be created (on the spot, even) only because they defend a previously held opinion. When someone is eager to share an opinion as if it were a conclusion, but looks puzzled or angry when asked for reasons, weak-sense critical thinking is the probable culprit.

Certainly, you have a large set of initial beliefs, which act as initial conclusions when you encounter controversies. As your respect for the importance of reasons grows, you will frequently expect those conclusions to stand or crumble on the basis of their support. Your strongest conclusions follow your reflection about the reasons and what they mean.

Be your own censor in this regard. You must shake your own pan when looking for gold. Try to avoid "reverse logic" or "backward reasoning," whereby reasons are an afterthought, following the selection of your conclusion. Ideally, reasons are the tool by which conclusions are shaped and modified.

## "Fresh" Reasons and Your Growth

We need to remind ourselves again and again how important it is to force ourselves to pay attention to "fresh" reasons, those that we have not previously considered. Being fair to such reasons is tough, but rewarding. What makes this task so difficult is our current opinions. They provide a starting point for our reaction to reasoning. We come to each conversation, essay, or lecture with a loyalty to the beliefs we already have. Thus our existing beliefs can be an obstacle to our listening and learning. But at another level we know there are thoughtful reasons that we have not yet encountered. For our personal growth we have to give "fresh" reasons a real chance to speak to us.

## Critical Thinking and Your Own Writing and Speaking

When you are writing or speaking, you will want to keep your audience fore-most in your plans. They need to be clear about what you conclude and why you are concluding it. Don't hide your conclusion and reasons; display them openly. Give the audience a clear opportunity to see what you intend. Thus, your task is to use words, sentences, paragraphs, and indicator words to illu-minate the logical relationships in your argument.

## Practice Exercises

 *Critical Question:* **What are the reasons?**

First survey the passage and highlight its conclusion. Then ask the question, "Why?" and locate the reasons. Use indicator words to help. Keep the conclu-sions and the reasons separate.

Passage 1

Divorce is on the increase, and we're worried. Finally, psychologists have identi-fied a key cause of divorce. Noticing that certain families have multiple divorces, they found that inherited genes play a major role in causing divorces.

Although the overall divorce rate is 20 percent, psychologists discovered that a twin has a 45 percent rate of divorce *if* the identical twin has already experienced a divorce. Additional confirming evidence for genes as a primary cause stems from looking at the divorce rate of twins' parents. If their parents have divorced, each twin has a 10 percent higher risk of divorce.

Passage 2

Speedy, colorful waterscooters are gaining in popularity. Waterscooters can travel anywhere a small boat can and are typically popular with young people. The rising popularity of the craft has raised the question of waterscooter regu-lation. In this case, the argument for strict regulation is compelling. Waterscooters are a particularly deadly form of water recreation.

For example, two women were vacationing in Longboat Key. While they were floating on a raft along the shore, a waterscooter crashed into them and killed them. Also, waterscooter operators have been killed or seriously injured in colli-sions with other watercraft. Others have been stranded at sea when their scooters either failed or sank far from shore. Many waterscooter operators are inexperi-enced and ignorant of navigational rules, increasing the potential for accidents.

In addition to the inherent operational hazards of waterscooters, they are proving to be an environmental nuisance. Beach residents complain of the intrusive noise of the scooters. The Pacific Whale Foundation on the West Coast expressed concern that the scooters are frightening away endangered humpback whales that migrate to Hawaii for breeding.

Regulations stipulating minimum operating age, restricted operating areas, and mandatory classes in water safety are essential. Without such regulations, tragedies involving waterscooters are sure to multiply, rendering many beaches unsafe for recreation.

Passage 3

Experience is widely recognized as being the best form of education. To experience a culture firsthand is the only way to truly understand how others live. It is often the most wealthy students who can afford to travel and experience foreign life, but if more students, particularly high school students, could travel, their plans for the future might include something beyond what dress to buy for the prom.

Schools should fund overseas travel to allow more students the opportunity to be educated through experience. Furthermore, these grants should not be given to those with the best GPAs because the experience of travel should be available to everyone. It is often the students who do not academically succeed in school who need life-changing experiences like travel to give them inspiration for plans for the future. School-funded travel gives young people the advantage of knowing about the global market in which they will soon need to function.

## Sample Responses

Passage 1

ISSUE: *What causes divorce?*

CONCLUSION: *Inherited genes are a major cause.*

REASONS:
1. *A twin whose twin has divorced a spouse has much greater than normal risk of also experiencing divorce.*
2. *When a twin's parents are divorced, the twin's risk of divorce shoots up by 10 percent.*

Recall that we are looking for the support system for the conclusion. We ask ourselves: Why does this person claim that genes play a major role in causing divorces? The conclusion is justified by two research findings; these findings constitute the reasons. Indicator words for the first and second reason are "psychologists found that" and "additional confirming evidence."

Passage 2

ISSUE:  *Should waterscooters be subject to strict regulation?*

CONCLUSION:  *Yes, waterscooters should be strictly regulated.*

REASONS:    1.  *Waterscooters are extremely dangerous.*

> (SUPPORTING REASONS)
>
> a.  *Operators are killing themselves and others.*
> b.  *Most waterscooter operators are inexperienced and ignorant of rules.*
> c.  *Crowding has worsened the problem.*

> 2.  *Waterscooters pose an environmental threat.*

> (SUPPORTING REASONS)
>
> a.  *The noise bothers beach residents.*
> b.  *Scooters may be scaring away endangered humpback whales.*

Why are we told that waterscooters should be strictly regulated? The answer to that question will be the author's reasons. The first reason is supported by a collection of examples and claims, all trying to make us aware of the extreme danger faced by those who dare to get on the waterscooters. *In addition* are the indicator words that call our attention to the second of the two reasons. That reason is the environmental hazard created by the unregulated use of the waterscooters. It has two supporting reasons. This passage is a good one for you to use to practice diagramming reasoning.

# CRITICAL QUESTION SUMMARY: WHY THIS QUESTION IS IMPORTANT

### What Are the Reasons?

Once you have identified the issue and conclusion, you need to understand *why* an author has come to a certain conclusion. Reasons are the *why*. If the author provides good reasons, you might be persuaded to accept her conclusion. However, right now, we are simply concerned with identifying the reasons. Identifying the reasons is the next step in deciding whether you should accept or reject the author's conclusion.

# WHAT WORDS OR PHRASES ARE AMBIGUOUS?

The first three chapters of this book help you identify the basic structural elements in any message. At this point, if you can locate a writer's or speaker's conclusion and reasons, you are progressing rapidly toward the ultimate goal of forming your own rational decisions. Your next step is to put this structural picture into even clearer focus.

While identifying the conclusion and reasons gives you the basic visible structure, you still need to examine the precise *meaning* of these parts before you can react fairly to the ideas being presented. You need now to pay much more attention to the details of the language.

Identifying the precise meaning of key words or phrases is an essential step in deciding whether to agree with someone's opinion. If you fail to check for the meaning of crucial terms and phrases, you may react to an opinion the author never intended.

Let's see why knowing the meaning of a communicator's terms is so important.

As we experience more and more of the effects of what seems to be global warming, we need to consider restrictions on our current way of life. Unless we stop living the way we have been living, we will surely drown as the oceans get larger and larger from the melting of the ice cap.

Notice that it is very hard to know what to think about this argument until we know more about the kinds of restrictions that the person has in mind. A fine is a restriction; so is the shutting down of major industries. We just do not know what to think until we know more about the restrictions the person is suggesting.

This example illustrates an important point: You cannot react to an argument unless you understand the meanings (explicit or implied) of crucial terms and phrases. How these are interpreted will often affect the acceptability of the reasoning. Consequently, before you can determine the extent to which you wish to accept one conclusion or another, you must first attempt to discover the precise meaning of the conclusion and the reasons. While their meaning typically *appears* obvious, it often is not.

The discovery and clarification of meaning require conscious, step-by-step procedures. This chapter suggests one set of such procedures. It focuses on the following question:

[?]   *Critical Question:* **What words or phrases are ambiguous?**

## The Confusing Flexibility of Words

Our language is highly complex. If each word had only one potential meaning about which we all agreed, effective communication would be more likely. However, most words have more than one meaning.

Consider the multiple meanings of such words as *freedom, obscenity,* and *happiness.* These multiple meanings can create serious problems in determining the worth of an argument. For example, when someone argues that a magazine should not be published because it is *obscene,* you cannot evaluate the argument until you know what the writer means by "obscene." In this brief argument, it is easy to find the conclusion and the supporting reason, but the quality of the reasoning is difficult to judge because of the ambiguous use of *obscene.* Thus, even when you can identify the basic structure of what others are saying, you still must struggle with the meaning of certain words in that structure. A warning: *We often misunderstand what we read or hear because we presume that the meaning of words is obvious.*

Whenever you are reading or listening, force yourself to *search for ambiguity;* otherwise, you may simply miss the point. A term or phrase is ambiguous when its meaning is so uncertain in the context of the argument we are examining that we need further clarification before we can judge the adequacy of the reasoning.

## Locating Key Terms and Phrases

The first step in determining which terms or phrases are ambiguous is to use the stated issue as a clue for possible key terms. Key terms or phrases will be those terms that may have more than one plausible meaning within the context of the issue; that is, terms that you know must be clarified before you can decide to agree or disagree with the communicator. To illustrate the potential benefit of checking terminology in the issue, let's examine several stated issues:

1.  Does TV violence adversely affect society?
2.  Is the Miss America contest demeaning to women?
3.  Is the incidence of rape in college residence halls increasing?

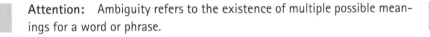

**Attention:**   Ambiguity refers to the existence of multiple possible meanings for a word or phrase.

Each of these stated issues contains phrases that writers or speakers will have to make clear before you will be able to evaluate their response to the issue. Each of the following phrases is potentially ambiguous: "TV violence," "adversely affect society," "demeaning to women," "incidence of rape." Thus, when you read an essay responding to these issues, you will want to pay close attention to how the author has defined these terms.

The next step in determining which terms or phrases are ambiguous is to identify what words or phrases seem crucial in determining how well the author's reasons support his conclusion; that is, to identify the *key* terms in the reasoning structure. Once you locate these terms, you can then determine whether their meaning is ambiguous.

When searching for key terms and phrases, you should keep in mind why you are looking. Someone wants you to accept a conclusion. Therefore, you are looking for only those terms or phrases that will affect whether you accept the conclusion. *So, look for them in the reasons and conclusion.* Terms and phrases that are not included in the basic reasoning structure can thus be "dumped from your pan."

Another useful guide for searching for key terms and phrases is to keep in mind the following rule: The more abstract a word or phrase, the more likely it is to be susceptible to multiple interpretations and thus need clear definition by the author. To avoid being unclear in our use of the term *abstract,* we define it here in the following way: A term becomes more and more abstract as it refers less and less to particular, specific instances. Thus, the words *equality, responsibility, pornography,* and *aggression* are much more abstract than are the phrases "having equal access to necessities of life," "directly causing an event," "pictures of male and female genitals," and "doing deliberate physical harm to another person." These phrases provide a much more concrete picture and are therefore less ambiguous.

You can also locate potential important ambiguous phrases by *reverse role-playing.* That is, ask yourself, if you were to *adopt a position contrary to the author's,* would you choose to define certain terms or phrases differently? If so, you have identified a possible ambiguity. For example, someone who sees beauty pageants as desirable is likely to define "demeaning to women" quite differently from someone who sees them as undesirable.

---

### Summary of Clues for Locating Key Terms

1.   Review the issue for possible key terms.
2.   Look for crucial words or phrases within the reasons and conclusion.
3.   Keep an eye out for abstract words and phrases.
4.   Use reverse role-playing to determine how someone might define certain words and phrases differently.

---

## Checking for Ambiguity

You now know where to look for those terms or phrases that are ambiguous. The next step is to focus on each term or phrase and ask yourself, "Do I understand its meaning?" In answering this very important question, you will need to overcome several major obstacles.

One obstacle is assuming that you and the author mean the same thing. Thus, you need to begin your search by avoiding "mind reading." You need to get into the habit of asking, "What do you mean by that?" instead of, "I know just what you mean." A second obstacle is assuming that terms have a single, obvious definition. Many terms do not. Thus, always ask, "Could any of the words or phrases have a different meaning?"

You can be certain you have identified an especially important unclear term by performing the following test. If you can express two or more alternative meanings for a term, each of which makes sense in the context of the argument, and if the extent to which a reason would support a conclusion is affected by which meaning is assumed, then you have located a significant ambiguity. Thus, a good test for determining whether you have identified an important ambiguity is to *substitute* the alternative meanings into the reasoning structure and see whether changing the meaning *makes a difference* in how well a reason supports the conclusion.

## USING THIS CRITICAL QUESTION

The preceding paragraph deserves your full attention. It is spelling out a procedure for putting this critical question about ambiguity to work. Once you have followed the procedure, you can demonstrate to yourself or anyone else why the reasoning needs more work. Try as you might to want to believe what is being said, you just cannot, as a critical thinker, agree with the reasoning until the ambiguity that affects the reasoning is repaired.

### Determining Ambiguity

Let's now apply the above hints to help us determine which key terms a communicator has not made sufficiently clear. Remember: As we do this exercise, keep asking, "What does the author mean by that?" and pay particular attention to abstract terms.

We will start with a simple reasoning structure: an advertisement.

*Lucky Smokes put it all together and got taste with only 3 mg. tar.*

ISSUE: *What cigarette should you buy?*

CONCLUSION: (implied): *Buy Lucky Smokes.*

REASON: *They got taste with only 3 mg. tar.*

The phrases "Buy Lucky Smokes" and "3 mg. tar" seem quite concrete and self-evident. But, how about "got taste?" Is the meaning obvious? We think not. How do we know? Let's perform a test together. Could "taste" have more than one meaning? Yes. It could mean a barely noticeable mild tobacco flavor. It could mean a rather harsh, bitter flavor. Or it could have many other meanings. Isn't it true that you would be more eager to follow the advice of the advertisement if the taste provided matched your taste preference? Thus, the ambiguity is significant because it affects the degree to which you might be persuaded by the ad.

Advertising is often full of ambiguity. Advertisers intentionally engage in ambiguity to persuade you that their products are superior to those of their competitors. Here are some sample advertising claims that are ambiguous. See if you can identify alternative, plausible meanings for the italicized words or phrases.

> No-Pain is the *extra-strength* pain reliever.
>
> Vanmusk Perfume: Just a step beyond your *dreams.*
>
> Ray Rhinestone's new album: an album of *experiences.*
>
> Vital Hair Vitamins show you *what* vitamins can do for your hair.
>
> Here is a book at last that shows you how to find and keep a *good man.*

In each case, the advertiser hoped that you would assign the most attractive meaning to the ambiguous words. Critical reading can sometimes protect you from making purchasing decisions that you would later regret.

Let's now look at a more complicated example of ambiguity. Remember to begin by identifying the issue, conclusion, and reasons. Resist the temptation to make note of the unclear meaning of any and all words. Only the ambiguity **in the reasoning** is crucial to critical thinkers.

> It is time to take active steps in reducing the amount of violence on television. The adverse effect of such violence is clear, as evidenced by many recent research studies. Several studies indicate that heavy TV watchers tend to overestimate the danger of physical violence in real life. Other studies show that children who are heavy TV watchers can become desensitized to violence in the real world. Numerous other studies demonstrate the adverse effects of TV violence.

This essay addresses the issue, should we do something about the violence on television? It concludes that we ought to take active steps to reduce the amount of TV violence, and the author's main reason supporting the conclusion is that such violence has an adverse effect. The writer then uses research evidence to support this reasoning. Let's examine the reasoning for any words or phrases that would affect our willingness to accept it.

First, let's examine the issue for terms we will want the author to make clear. Certainly, we would not be able to agree or disagree with this author's conclusion until she has indicated what she means by "violence on television." Thus, we will want to check how clearly she has defined it in her reasoning.

Next, let's list all key terms and phrases in the conclusion and reasons: "take active steps in reducing the amount of violence on television," "adverse effect," "many recent research studies," "several studies," "heavy TV watchers," "tend to overestimate the danger of physical violence in real life," "other studies," "children who are heavy TV watchers," "can become desensitized to violence in the real world," "numerous other studies," "demonstrate," "adverse effect of TV violence." Let's take a close look at a few of these to determine whether they could have different meanings that might make a difference in how we would react to the reasoning.

First, her conclusion is ambiguous. Exactly what does it mean to "take active steps in reducing the amount of violence"? Does it mean to impose a legal ban against showing any act of physical violence, or might it mean putting public pressure on the networks to restrict violent episodes to late evening hours? Before you could decide whether to agree with the speaker or writer, you would first have to decide what it is she wants us to believe.

Next, she argues that "heavy" TV watchers "overestimate the danger of physical violence in real life" and "become desensitized to violence in the real world." But how much TV does one have to watch to qualify as a heavy TV watcher? Perhaps most people are not heavy TV watchers, given the actual research study's definition of that phrase. If so, then the reason would not be very supportive of the conclusion because it would not be relevant to most TV watchers. Also, what does it mean to overestimate the danger of physical violence, or to become desensitized? Try to create a mental picture of what these phrases represent. If you can't, the phrases are ambiguous. If different images would cause you to react to the reasons differently, you have identified an important ambiguity.

Now, check the other phrases we listed above. Do they not also need to be clarified? You can see that if you accept this writer's argument without requiring her to clarify these ambiguous phrases, you will not have understood what it is you agreed to believe.


## Context and Ambiguity

Writers and speakers only rarely define their terms. Thus, typically your only guide to the meaning of an ambiguous statement is the context in which the words are used. By *context,* we mean the writer's or speaker's background, traditional uses of the term within the particular controversy, and the words and statements preceding and following the possible ambiguity. All three elements provide clues to the meaning of a potential key term or phrase.

If you were to see the term *human rights* in an essay, you should immediately ask yourself, "What rights are those?" If you examine the context and find that the writer is a leading member of the Norwegian government, it is a good bet that the human rights he has in mind are the rights to be employed, receive free health care, and obtain adequate housing. An American senator might mean something very different by human rights. She could have in mind freedoms of speech, religion, travel, and peaceful assembly. Notice that the two versions of human rights are not necessarily consistent. A country could guarantee one form of human rights and at the same time violate the other. You must try to clarify such terms by examining their context.

Writers frequently make clear their assumed meaning for a term by their arguments. The following paragraph is an example:

> Studies show that most people who undergo psychotherapy benefit from the experience. In fact, a recent study shows that after ten sessions of psychotherapy, two-thirds of participants reported experiencing less anxiety.

The phrase "benefit from the experience" is potentially ambiguous, because it could have a variety of meanings. However, the writer's argument makes clear that in this context, "benefit from the experience" means reporting less anxiety.

Note that, even in this case, you would want some further clarification before you call a therapist, because "reporting less anxiety" is ambiguous. Wouldn't you want to know how *much* lowering of anxiety was experienced? Perhaps participants still experienced significant amounts of anxiety—but less than previously.

A major advantage of recognizing that terms or phrases may have multiple meanings is that locating the author's meaning offers the option of *disagreeing* with it. If you disagree with a debatable, assumed definition, then you will want to recognize that the quality of the author's reasoning is conditional upon the definition used, and you will not want to be unduly influenced by the reasoning. Thus, in the above example you may believe that a preferred definition of "benefits of psychotherapy" is "a major restructuring of personality characteristics." If so, *for you,* the author's reason would not be supportive of the conclusion.

## USING THIS CRITICAL QUESTION

The critical question focusing on ambiguity provides you with a fair-minded basis for disagreeing with the reasoning. If you and the person trying to persuade you are using different meanings for key terms in the reasoning, you would have to work out those disagreements first before you could accept the reasoning being offered to you.

*Examine the context carefully* to determine the meaning of key terms and phrases. If the meaning remains uncertain, you have located an important ambiguity. If the meaning is clear and you disagree with it, then you should be wary of any reasoning that involves that term or phrase.

## Ambiguity, Definitions, and the Dictionary

It should be obvious from the preceding discussion that to locate and clarify ambiguity, you must be aware of the possible meanings of words. Meanings usually come in one of three forms: synonyms, examples, and what we will call "definition by specific criteria." For example, one could offer at least three different definitions of *anxiety:*

1.  Anxiety is feeling nervous. (*synonym*)
2.  Anxiety is what the candidate experienced when he turned on the television to watch the election returns. (*example*)
3.  Anxiety is a subjective feeling of discomfort accompanied by increased sensitivity of the autonomic nervous system. (*specific criteria*)

For critical evaluation of most controversial issues, synonyms and examples are inadequate. They fail to tell you the specific properties that are crucial for an unambiguous understanding of the term. Useful definitions are those that specify criteria for usage—and the more specific the better.

Where do you go for your definitions? One obvious and very important source is your dictionary. However, dictionary definitions frequently consist of synonyms, examples, or incomplete specifications of criteria for usage. These definitions often do not adequately define the use of a term in a particular essay. In such cases, you must discover possible meanings from the context of the passage, or from what else you know about the topic. We suggest you keep a dictionary handy, but keep in mind that the appropriate definition may not be there.

Let's take a closer look at some of the inadequacies of a dictionary definition. Examine the following brief paragraph.

> The quality of education at this university is not declining. In my interviews, I found that an overwhelming majority of the students and instructors responded that they saw no decline in the quality of education here.

It is clearly important to know what is meant by "quality of education" in the preceding paragraph. If you look up the word *quality* in the dictionary, you will find many meanings, the most appropriate, given this context, being *excellence* or *superiority*. *Excellence* and *superiority* are synonyms for quality—and they are equally abstract. You still need to know precisely what is meant by *excellence* or *superiority*. How do you know whether education is high in quality or excellence? Ideally, you would want the writer to tell you precisely what *behaviors* he is referring to when he uses the phrase "quality of education." Can you think of some different ways that the phrase might be defined? The following list presents some possible definitions of *quality of education:*

average grade-point average of students

ability of students to think critically

number of professors who have doctoral degrees

amount of work usually required to pass an exam

Each of these definitions suggests a different way to measure quality; each specifies a different criterion. Each provides a concrete way in which the term could be used. Note also that each of these definitions will affect the degree to which you will want to agree with the author's reasoning. For example, if you believe that "quality" should refer to the ability of students to think critically, and most of the students in the interviews are defining it as how much work is required to pass an exam, the reason would not *necessarily* support the conclusion. Exams may not require the ability to think critically.

Thus, in many arguments you will not be able to find adequate dictionary definitions, and the context may not make the meaning clear. One way to discover possible alternative meanings is to try to create a mental picture of what the words represent. If you cannot do so, then you probably have identified an important ambiguity. Let's apply such a test to the following example:

Attending college has the effect of creating better citizens. Thus, it is disappointing to see how state legislators, supported by voters, keep raising the tuition for prospective students. Do they know some secret, cheap technique for achieving a strong democracy that makes college unnecessary?

The standard used in this argument to assess the behavior of state legislators when they raise college tuition is the effect of college on *creating better citizens.* Can you create a single clear mental picture of a high quality "citizen"? We each have some such idea, but it is highly unlikely that the ideas are identical; indeed, they may be quite different. Does "better citizens" refer to greater engagement in the local community or to increased literacy or to something else entirely? For us to evaluate the argument, we would need to know more about the meaning the writer has for "better citizens." Thus, we have located an important ambiguity.

## Ambiguity and Loaded Language

Ambiguity is not always an accident. Those trying to persuade you are often quite aware that words have multiple meanings. Furthermore, they know that certain of those meanings carry with them heavy emotional baggage. Words like *sacrifice* and *justice* have multiple meanings, and some of those meanings are loaded in the sense that they stimulate certain emotions in us. Anyone trying to use language to lead us by the heart can take advantage of these probable emotions.

Political language is often loaded and ambiguous. For example, *welfare* is often how we refer to governmental help to those we don't like; when help from the government goes to groups we like, we call it a *subsidy* or an *incentive*. The following table consists of political terms and the intended emotional impact.

| Ambiguous Political Language | |
| --- | --- |
| Term | Emotional Impact |
| Revenue enhancement | Positive response to tax hikes |
| Tax and spend democrats | Irresponsible and wasteful |
| Restoring fairness | Approval of proposed tax changes |
| Extreme | Undesirable, unreasonable |
| Terrorist | Wild, crazy, uncivilized |
| Defense spending | Protective, required |
| Reform | Desirable changes |

All the terms in the table are ambiguous. As critical thinkers, we must be sensitive to their intended emotional impact and the role of ambiguity in encouraging that impact. By searching for alternative meanings of terms such as *reform,* we can safeguard ourselves against easy emotional commitments to arguments we would otherwise question. After all, even the most dangerous political change is in some sense a "reform."

Norman Solomon's *The Power of Babble* provides a colorful illustration of how successful politicians use ambiguous language to persuade others. Note that Mr. Solomon has conveniently placed key ambiguous terms in alphabetical order for us.

America is back, and bipartisan—biting the bullet with competitiveness, diplomacy, efficiency, empowerment, end games, and environmentalism, along with faith in the founding Fathers, freedom's blessings, free markets and free peoples, and most of all, God. Our great heritage has held the line for human rights, individual initiative, justice, kids, leadership, liberty, loyalty, mainstream values, the marketplace, measured responses, melting pots, the middle class, military reform, moderates, modernization, moral standards, national security, and Old Glory. Opportunity comes from optimism, patriotism, peace through strength, the people, pluralism, and points of light. Pragmatism and the power of prayer make for principle while the private sector protects the public interest. Realism can mean recycling, self-discipline, and the spirit of '76, bring stability and standing tall for strategic interests and streamlined taxation. Uncle Sam has been undaunted ever since Valley Forge, with values venerated by veterans; vigilance, vigor, vision, voluntarism, and Western values. (page 3)

## Limits of Your Responsibility to Clarify Ambiguity

After you have attempted to identify and clarify ambiguity, what can you do if you are still uncertain about the meaning of certain key ideas? What is a reasonable next step? We suggest you ignore any reason containing ambiguity that makes it impossible to judge the acceptability of the reason. It is your responsibility as an active learner to ask questions that clarify ambiguity. However, your responsibility stops at that point. It is the writer or speaker who is trying to convince you of something. Her role as a persuader requires her to respond to your concerns about possible ambiguity.

You are not required to react to ideas or options that are unclear. If a friend tells you that you should enroll in a class because it "really is different," but cannot tell you how it is different, then you have no basis for agreeing or disagreeing with the advice. No one has the right to be believed if he cannot provide you with a clear picture of his reasoning.

## Ambiguity and Your Own Writing and Speaking

Although most of this chapter is addressed to you as a critical reader and listener, it is also extremely relevant to improved writing and speaking. Effective communicators strive for clarity. They review what they intend to say several times, looking for any statements that might be ambiguous.

Look back at the section on "Locating Key Terms and Phrases" (page 39). Use the hints given there for finding important ambiguity to revise your own efforts to communicate. For instance, abstractions that are ambiguous can be clarified by providing specific criteria for the use of the abstraction or clarify by concrete illustrations, conveying the meaning you intend. Pay special attention to your own reasons and conclusions; try to rid them of ambiguity out of respect for your audience. When you fear ambiguity of expression, carefully define your terms.

Thinking about the characteristics of your intended audience can help you decide where ambiguities need to be clarified. A specialized audience may adequately understand jargon or specific abstractions that would be very ambiguous to a general audience. Remember that your audience will probably not struggle for a long time with your meaning. If you confuse a member of your audience, you will probably lose her quickly. If you never regain her attention, then you have failed in your task as a communicator.

Take another look at the previous section discussing the burden of responsibility surrounding the use of ambiguity. It is you the writer or speaker who must bear that burden; it is you who is attempting to convince someone else.

## Summary

You cannot evaluate an essay until you know the communicator's intended meaning of key terms and phrases as well as alternative meanings they could conceivably have had in the context of the argument. You can find important clues to potential ambiguity in the statement of the issue and can locate key words and phrases in the reasons and confusions. Because many authors fail to define their terms and because many key terms have multiple meanings, you must search for possible ambiguity. You do this by asking the questions, "What *could* be meant?" and "What *is* meant by the key terms?" Once you have completed the search, you will know four very important components of the reasoning:

1. the key terms and phrases,
2. which of these are adequately defined,
3. which of these possess other possible definitions, which if substituted, would modify your reaction to the reasoning, and
4. which of these are ambiguous within the context of the argument.

## Practice Exercises

[?]  *Critical Question:* **What words or phrases are ambiguous?**

In the following passages, identify examples of ambiguity. Try to explain why the examples harm the reasoning.

Passage 1

We should treat drug use in the same way we treat speech and religion, as a fundamental right. No one has to ingest any drug he does not want, just as no one has to read a particular book. Insofar as the state, the only reason the state assumes control over such matters, is to subjugate its citizens—by protecting them from temptations as befits children, and by preventing them from exercising self-determination over their lives as befits slaves.

Passage 2

We categorically disapprove the theory, apparently adopted by the trial judge, that obscene, pornographic films acquire constitutional immunity from state regulation simply because they are exhibited for consenting adults only. This holding was properly rejected by the Georgia Supreme Court. . . . In particular, we hold that there are legitimate state interests at stake in stemming the tide of commercialized obscenity, even assuming it is feasible to enforce effective safeguards against exposure to juveniles and passersby. Rights and interests other than those of the advocates are involved. These include the interest of the public in the quality of life and the total community environment, the tone of commerce in the great city centers, and possibly, the public safety itself . . .

As Chief Justice Warren stated, there is a "right of the Nation and of the States to maintain a decent society . . . ," *Jacobellis v. Ohio*, 378 U.S. 184, 199 (1964) (dissenting opinion) . . .

The sum of experience, including that of the past two decades, affords an ample basis for legislatures to conclude that a sensitive, key relationship of human existence, central to family life, community welfare and the development of human personality, can be debased and distorted by crass commercial exploitation of sex.

Note: This passage is adapted from an opinion delivered by Chief Justice Warren Burger in a Supreme Court response concerning the constitutionality of a Georgia obscenity statute.

Passage 3

Sugary cereal is the downfall of many of us. Brightly colored boxes with marshmallows and colored rice puffs are what far too many of us are eating for breakfast.

Often times, these cereals have no more nutrition than a candy bar! This is not the proper way to send kids off to school. It is extremely difficult to focus in school when one has eaten a bowl full of sugar and chemicals. Research has shown that children who eat a healthy, organic breakfast earn better grades in school.

In addition, adults report feeling more ready for the day and more efficient at work when they eat a healthy breakfast.

## Sample Responses

### Passage 1

ISSUE: *Should the state regulate drug use?*

CONCLUSION: *Drug use should not be regulated by the state.*

REASONS:    1. *Just as freedom of speech and religion, drug use is a fundamental right.*

          2. *State control subjugates citizens by not permitting them to take responsibility for voluntary acts.*

What are the key phrases in this reasoning? They are: "drug use," "fundamental right," and "subjugate citizens." You would first want to determine the meaning of each of these phrases. Is it clear what is meant by drug use? No. The limited context provided fails to reveal an adequate definition. If drug use refers to the ingestion of drugs that are not considered highly addictive, such as marijuana, wouldn't you be more likely to accept the reasoning than if the author included heroin within his definition of drugs? Can you tell from the argument whether the author is referring to all drugs or only to a subset of currently regulated drugs? To be able to agree or to disagree with the author requires in this instance a more careful definition of what is meant by "drug use." Notice that "fundamental right" and "subjugate citizens" need further clarification before you can decide whether to agree with the author.

### Passage 2

ISSUE: *Does the state have the right to regulate obscene materials?*

CONCLUSION: *Yes.*

REASONS:    1. *The nation and the states have a right to maintain a decent society.*

          2. *Experience proves that crass commercial exploitation of sex debases and distorts sexual relationships.*

The issue and conclusion jointly inform us that we are going to need to know what the author means by obscene materials before we can decide whether we want to agree with his arguments. Because the context we are given fails to clearly specify the meaning of "obscene," we find it difficult to agree or disagree with the conclusion. Obscenity can have so many plausible meanings. For example, we might react differently to a definition emphasizing nudity than to a definition emphasizing perversity in sexual behavior. Thus obscenity is an important ambiguity in the context of this essay.

Several key phrases within the reasoning structure need clarification before we can evaluate the reasoning. Certainly, "maintaining a decent society" can have multiple meanings, and the author's reference to quality of life and total community environment, tone of commerce, and public safety is not as helpful as we would like. Given this language we would have a difficult time determining whether showing pornographic films "debases society." In fact, some might argue that restricting the right to show such films "debases society," because it restricts a "freedom."

We have a similar problem regarding the second reason. What is the meaning of debasing and distorting a sensitive key relationship? We think there are multiple plausible meanings, some that might be consistent with the impact of pornography and some that might not be.

## CRITICAL QUESTION SUMMARY: WHY THIS QUESTION IS IMPORTANT

### What Words or Phrases Are Ambiguous?

Once you have identified an author's argument, you need to identify key words or phrases within that reasoning that might have alternative meanings. More importantly, you need to determine whether the author explicitly uses one of those definitions. If she does not, and if one of those meanings alters your acceptance of the conclusion, you have identified an important ambiguity. Identifying ambiguous words and phrases is the next important step in determining whether you will accept or reject the conclusion.

# 5

# WHAT ARE THE VALUE CONFLICTS AND ASSUMPTIONS?

Anyone trying to convince you to believe a particular position will make an attempt to present reasons consistent with that position. Hence, at first glance almost every argument appears to "make sense." The visible structure looks good. But the visible, stated reasons are not the only ideas that serve to prove or support the conclusion. Hidden or unstated beliefs may be at least as significant in understanding the argument. Let's examine the importance of these unstated ideas by considering the following brief argument.

> The government should prohibit the manufacture and sale of cigarettes. More and more evidence has demonstrated that smoking has harmful effects on the health of both the smoker and those exposed to smoking.

The reason—at first glance—supports the conclusion. If the government wants to prohibit a product, it makes sense that it should provide evidence that the product is bad. But it is also possible that the reason given can be true and yet not *necessarily* support the conclusion. What if you believe that it is the individual's responsibility—not the collective responsibility of government—to take care of his or her own welfare? If so, from your perspective, the reason no longer supports the conclusion. This reasoning is convincing to you only if you agree with certain unstated ideas that the writer has taken for granted. In this case, one idea taken for granted is that collective responsibility is more desirable than individual responsibility when an individual's welfare is threatened.

In all arguments, there will be certain ideas taken for granted by the writer. Typically, these ideas will not be stated. You will have to find them by reading between the lines. These ideas are important invisible links in the reasoning structure, the glue that holds the entire argument together. Until you supply these links, you cannot truly understand the argument.

If you miss the hidden links, you will often find yourself believing something that had you been more reflective, you would never have accepted. Remember: the visible surface of an argument will almost always be dressed in its best clothes because the person presenting the argument wishes to encourage you to make the argument your own. This chapter can be particularly useful to you as a critical thinker because it prepares you to look at the full argument, not just its more attractive features.

Your task is similar in many ways to having to reproduce a magic trick without having seen how the magician did the trick. You see the handkerchief go into the hat and the rabbit come out, but you are not aware of the magician's hidden maneuvers. To understand the trick, you must discover these maneuvers. Likewise, in arguments, you must discover the hidden maneuvers, which, in actuality, are unstated ideas. We shall refer to these unstated ideas as assumptions. To fully understand an argument, you must identify the assumptions.

Assumptions are:

1. hidden or unstated (in most cases),
2. taken for granted,
3. influential in determining the conclusion, and
4. potentially deceptive.

This chapter and the next one will show you how to discover assumptions. We will focus on one kind of assumption in this chapter—value assumptions.

But identifying assumptions is more valuable than just the positive impact it has on your own reasoning. Critical thinking necessarily involves other people who are concerned about the same issues as you. When you identify assumptions and make them explicit in your interactions with others, you make a tremendous contribution to the quality of the reasoning in our community as well. You are thereby making explicit the positive effect of critical thinking in a democracy.

*Critical Question:* **What are the value conflicts and assumptions?**

## General Guide for Identifying Assumptions

When you seek assumptions, where and how should you look? Numerous assumptions exist in any book, discussion, or article, but you need to be concerned about relatively few. As you remember, the visible structure of an argument consists of reasons and conclusions. Thus, you are interested only in assumptions that affect the quality of this structure. You can restrict your search for assumptions, therefore, to the structure you have already learned how to identify.

In particular, there are two places to look for assumptions. Look for assumptions needed for the reason(s) to support the conclusions (linkage assumptions) and look for ones necessary for a reason to be true. We first introduce you to assumptions that are extremely influential in prescriptive arguments—value assumptions. **Look for value assumptions in the movement from reasons to conclusion!**

Note that the reasons and conclusion are also the place where we search for significant ambiguity. Once again, we are showing great respect for the importance in a speech or essay of the reasons and the conclusion.

 **Attention:** An assumption is an unstated belief that supports the explicit reasoning.

## Value Conflicts and Assumptions

Why is it that some very reasonable people shout that abortion is murder, while other equally reasonable observers see abortion as humane? Have you ever wondered why every U.S. president, regardless of his political beliefs, eventually gets involved in a dispute with the press over publication of government information that he would prefer not to share? How can some highly intelligent observers attack the publication of sexually explicit magazines and others defend their publication as the ultimate test of our Bill of Rights?

One extremely important reason for these different conclusions is the existence of *value conflicts*, or the differing values that stem from different frames of reference. For ethical or prescriptive arguments, an individual's values influence the reasons he provides and, consequently, his conclusion. In fact, the reasons will logically support the conclusion only if the *value assumption* is added to the reasoning. The small argument below illustrates the role of a value assumption in a prescriptive argument.

> We should not legalize recreational drugs. Illegal drugs cause too much street violence and other crimes.

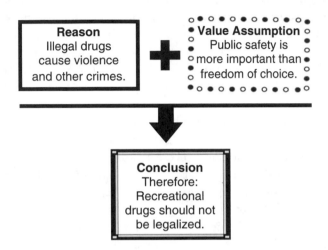

Value assumptions are very important assumptions for such arguments because they are directing the reasoning from behind a screen. The person trying to communicate with you may or may not be aware of these assumptions. You should make it a habit to identify the value assumptions on which the reasons are based.

By *value assumption* we mean a taken-for-granted belief about the *relative desirability* of certain competing values. When authors take a position on a social controversy, they typically prefer one value over another value—they have value *priorities or preferences.* The rest of this chapter is devoted to increasing your awareness of the role played by value conflicts and value priorities in determining a person's opinions or conclusions. This awareness will help you locate and evaluate this important type of assumption.

## Discovering Values

Before you can discover the importance of values in shaping conclusions, you must have some understanding of what a value is. *Values,* as we will use the term, are ideas that someone thinks are worthwhile. You will find that it is the importance one assigns to *abstract ideas* that has the major influence on one's choices and behavior.

Usually objects, experiences, and actions are desired because of some idea we value. For example, we may choose to do things that provide us with contacts with important people. We value "important people" (concrete idea) because we value "status" (abstract idea). When we use the word *value* in this chapter, we will be referring to an (abstract) idea representing what someone thinks is important and good.

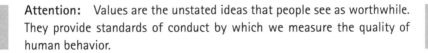

**Attention:**   Values are the unstated ideas that people see as worthwhile. They provide standards of conduct by which we measure the quality of human behavior.

To better familiarize yourself with values, write down some of your own values. Try to avoid writing down the names of people, tangible objects, or actions. Pizza and playing tennis may be important to you, but it is the importance you assign to abstract ideas that most influences your choices and behavior concerning controversial public issues. Your willingness to argue for or against capital punishment, for instance, is strongly related to the importance you assign to the sanctity of human life—an abstract idea. The sanctity of human life is a value that affects our opinions about war, abortion, drug usage, and mercy killing. As you create your list of values, focus on those that are so significant that they affect your opinions and behavior in many ways.

Did you have problems making your list? We can suggest two further aids that may help. First, another definition! Values are *standards of conduct* that we endorse and expect people to meet. When we expect our political representatives to "tell the truth," we are indicating to them and to ourselves that honesty is one of our most cherished values. Ask yourself what you expect your friends to be like. What standards of conduct would you want your children to develop? Answers to these questions should help you enlarge your understanding of values.

Now let us give you an aid for identifying values—a list of some commonly held values. Every value on our list may be an attractive candidate for your list. Thus, after you look at our list, pause for a moment and choose those values that are most important to you. They will be those values that most often play a role in shaping your opinions and behavior.

| Common Values | | |
| --- | --- | --- |
| adventure | equality of opportunity | patriotism |
| ambition | excellence | peace |
| autonomy | flexibility | rationality |
| collective responsibility | freedom of speech | security |
| comfort | generosity | spontaneity |
| competition | harmony | tolerance |
| cooperation | honesty | tradition |
| courage | justice | wisdom |
| creativity | novelty | |
| equality of condition | order | |

## From Values to Value Assumptions

To identify value assumptions, we must go beyond a simple listing of values. Others share many of your values. Wouldn't almost anyone claim that flexibility, cooperation, and honesty are desirable?

Look again at the definition, and you will immediately see that, *by definition,* most values will be on everyone's list. Because many values are shared, values by themselves are not a powerful guide to understanding. What leads you to answer a prescriptive question differently from someone else is the relative intensity with which you hold specific values.

That we attach different levels of intensity to specific values can be appreciated by thinking about responses to controversies when pairs of values collide or conflict. While it is not very enlightening to discover that most people value both competition and cooperation, we do gain a more complete understanding of prescriptive choices as we discover who *prefers* competition to cooperation when the two values conflict.

A writer's preference for particular values is often unstated, but that value preference, nevertheless, will have a major impact on her conclusion and on how she chooses to defend it. These unstated assertions about value priorities function as *value assumptions.* Some refer to these assumptions as *value judgments.* Recognition of relative support for conflicting values or sets of values provides you with both an improved understanding of what you are reading and a basis for eventual evaluation of prescriptive arguments.

When a writer takes a stand on controversial prescriptive issues, he is usually depreciating one commonly shared value while upholding another.

For example, when someone advocates the required licensing of prospective parents, collective responsibility is being treated as more important than individual responsibility. So when you look for value assumptions, look for an indication of value *priorities*. Ask yourself what values are being upheld by this position and what values are being relatively downgraded in importance.

**Attention:**   A value assumption is an implicit preference for one value over another in a particular context. We use value preferences and value priorities as synonyms.

When you have found a person's value preference in a particular argument, you should not expect that same person to necessarily have the same value priority when discussing a different controversy. A person does not have the same value priorities without regard to the issue being discussed. The context and factual issues associated with a controversy also greatly influence how far we're willing to go with a particular value preference. We hold our value preferences *only up to a point*. Thus, for example, those who prefer freedom of choice over the welfare of the community in most situations (such as wearing clothing that displays an image of the flag) may shift that value preference when they see the possibility of too much damage to the welfare of the community (such as in the case of the right of a person to give a racist speech.)

In other words, value assumptions are very contextual; they apply in one setting, but we may make quite a different value priority when the specifics of the prescriptive issue change. Critical thinking plays a major role in thinking deeply about whether we want to assign priority to particular values in a given instance.

## Typical Value Conflicts

If you are aware of typical conflicts, you can more quickly recognize the assumptions being made by a writer when she reaches a particular conclusion. We have listed some of the more common value conflicts that occur in ethical issues and have provided you with examples of controversies in which these value conflicts are likely to be evident. We anticipate that you can use this list as a starting point when you are trying to identify important value assumptions.

As you identify value conflicts, you will often find that there are several value conflicts that seem important in shaping conclusions with respect to particular controversies. When evaluating a controversy, try to find several value conflicts, as a check on yourself. Some controversies will have one primary value conflict; others may have several.

| Typical Value Conflict and Sample Controversies | |
| --- | --- |
| 1. loyalty–honesty | 1. Should you tell your parents about your sister's drug habit? |
| 2. competition–cooperation | 2. Do you support the grading system? |
| 3. freedom of press–national security | 3. Is it wise to hold weekly presidential press conferences? |
| 4. equality–individualism | 4. Are racial quotas for employment fair? |
| 5. order–freedom of speech | 5. Should we imprison those with radical ideas? |
| 6. security–excitement | 6. Should you choose a dangerous profession? |
| 7. generosity–material success | 7. Is it desirable to give financial help to a beggar? |
| 8. rationality–spontaneity | 8. Should you check the odds before placing a bet? |
| 9. tradition–novelty | 9. Should divorces be easily available? |

Take another look at number 7 in the preceding list. It is quite possible that value conflicts besides that between generosity and material success affect your decision about whether to give financial help to a beggar. For instance, all the following value conflicts may affect a person's willingness to help a beggar:

1. individual responsibility–collective responsibility
2. competition–cooperation
3. efficiency–social stability

By identifying as many of the relevant value assumptions as possible, you have a better chance of not missing any of the important dimensions of the argument. However, you may have no way of knowing which value assumptions most influence the author's reasoning.

## The Communicator's Background as a Clue to Value Assumptions

We suggested earlier that a good starting point in finding value assumptions is to check the background of the author. Find out as much as you can about the value preferences usually held by a person like the writer. Is he a corporate executive, a union leader, a Republican Party official, a doctor, or an apartment tenant? What interests does such a person naturally wish to protect? There's certainly nothing inherently wrong with pursuing self-interest, but such pursuits often limit the value assumptions a particular writer will tolerate. For example, it's highly unlikely that the president of a major automobile firm would place a high value on efficiency when a preference for efficiency rather than stability would lead to his losing his job. Consequently, you as a critical reader or listener can often quickly discover value preferences by thinking about the probable assumptions made by a person like the writer.

One caution is important. It isn't necessarily true that, because a writer is a member of a group, she shares the particular value assumptions of the group. It would be a mistake to presume that every individual who belongs to a given group thinks identically. We all know that business people, farmers, and firefighters sometimes disagree among themselves when discussing particular controversies. Investigating the writer's background as a clue to her value assumptions is only a clue, and, like other clues, it can be misleading unless it is used with care.

## Consequences as Clues to Value Assumptions

In prescriptive arguments, each position with respect to an issue leads to different consequences or outcomes. Each of the potential consequences will have a certain likelihood of occurring, and each will also have some level of desirability or undesirability. How desirable a consequence is will depend on a writer's or reader's personal value preferences. The desirability of the conclusions in such cases will be dictated by the probability of the potential consequences and the importance attached to them. Thus, an important means of determining an individual's value assumptions is to examine the reasons given in support of a conclusion and then to determine what value priorities would lead to these reasons being judged as more desirable than reasons that might have been offered on the other side of the issue. Let's take a look at a concrete example.

*Nuclear power plants should not be built because they will pollute our environment.*

The reason provided here is a rather specific potential consequence of building nuclear plants. This writer clearly sees environmental pollution as very undesirable. Why does this consequence carry so much weight in this person's thinking? What more general value does preventing pollution help achieve? We are only guessing, but probably health or conservation are being weighted especially heavily by this person. Someone else might stress a different consequence in this argument, such as the effect on the supply of electricity to consumers. Why? Probably because he values efficiency very highly! Thus, this reason supports the conclusion *if* a value assumption is made that conservation is more important than efficiency.

Note that the *magnitude* of a consequence may have a major impact on value preferences. One may value conservation over efficiency only when efficiency may cause "significant" damage to the environment. And, one may value economic freedom over economic security only as long as unemployment stays below a given level. It is possible for people to have different conclusions, while having identical value assumptions, because they disagree about the likelihood or magnitude of consequences.

One important means of determining value assumptions, then, is to ask the question, "Why do the particular consequences or outcomes presented as reasons seem so desirable to the writer or speaker?"

*Remember:* When you identify *value assumptions,* you should always try to state *value priorities.* With controversial topics, stating value assumptions in this way will be a continual reminder both of what the writer is *giving up* and of what she is gaining. Try to resist the temptation to stop your analysis prematurely by just identifying the values of the speaker or writer. Identifying those values is a step on the way to finding the value assumptions, but by itself it provides very little assistance in understanding an argument. Values, by their nature, are possessed by us all.

## More Hints for Finding Value Assumptions

Another useful technique for generating value conflicts is to *reverse role-play.* Ask the question, "What do those people who would take a different position from the writer's care about?" When someone argues that we should not use monkeys in experimental research, you should ask yourself, "If I wanted to defend the use of monkeys, what would I be concerned about?" Remember, when someone takes a position on a controversial topic, she will be revealing a *value priority*—a *preference for one value over another.* Your knowledge of that preference will help you to decide whether to agree with her conclusion.

Finally, you can always check to see whether the disagreement results from a value conflict concerning the *rights of an individual* to behave in a particular fashion and the *welfare of the group* affected by the behavior in question. Many arguments rest implicitly on a stance with respect to this enduring value conflict. Like other common value conflicts, we can all recall numerous instances when our thinking required us to weigh these two important values and their effects.

For example, when we wonder about the merit of mandatory drug-testing in the workplace, we often begin to construct our arguments in terms of thinking about the privacy rights of the individual workers *and* the threats to the community that might result from a worker's drug-related judgment error. Then, we try to balance those values: Does the individual's right to privacy deserve greater protection than the welfare of the community in this instance? What other issues involve this value conflict? What about the request of "skinheads" to parade through ethnic neighborhoods?

---

### Clues for Identifying Value Assumptions

1. Investigate the author's background.

2. Ask "Why do the consequences of the author's position seem so important to him or her?"

3. Search for similar social controversies to find analogous value assumptions.

4. Use reverse role-playing. Take a position opposite the author's position and identify which values are important to that opposite position.

5. Look for common value conflicts, such as individual responsibility versus community responsibility.

---

## Avoiding a Typical Difficulty When Identifying Value Assumptions

One common problem experienced by those who begin searching for value assumptions can be avoided. Let us explain the problem by using the following small prescriptive argument:

> Cities built in the desert, like Phoenix and Las Vegas, work hard to attract tourists and the jobs those tourists create. The economic wellbeing of current residents is greatly enhanced by making the cities more attractive to new business.
>
> To make their cities more attractive, the price of water in those cities is often cheaper than the price of water in areas of the country where water is abundant.

So it is quite common to see beautiful green lawns in these desert locations. The idea that we would reduce the limited supply of water and thereby deny future generations an adequate supply of water is a disgrace that we should repair.

Suppose you read the argument and then say: I believe the person values water and the future. At one level, you have identified what the person who made the argument sees as important. She does indicate a desire to have adequate water for future generations. But that response is too concrete to serve as an avenue toward deeper thinking about this prescriptive issue.

To move in a more productive way toward a better understanding of the issue, take another look at the definition of values. That definition suggests a need to place future generations and water into a more abstract framework. Once that need is recognized, a common response is to say: She values conservation and intergenerational empathy. That recognition is a step in the right direction. Conservation and intergenerational empathy ARE at work in this argument propelling the reasoning. Those same values are relevant to any number of issues surrounding air quality and endangered species as well. But we still are not at the most revealing level of value assumptions.

In that values are in tension with one another, we are missing a lot when we just call out values a person has. Their relative ranking when compared to other values that affect this argument is what assists in determining the person's conclusions. That they value conservation over economic development or intergenerational empathy over personal liberty is what pushes so hard in the direction of frowning on the low price of water in desert communities.

So push yourself all the way to finding value assumptions. Don't stop your search at levels of analysis that are less revealing.

## Finding Value Assumptions on Your Own

Let's work on an example together to help you become more comfortable with finding value assumptions.

Congress is attempting to pass legislation that will reduce the level of commercial exploitation currently present in children's television programming. The proposal calls for limitations on the number and types of commercials permitted during children's programs. This proposal has met with great opposition from those who insist that parents, not legislators, should monitor television viewing. They maintain that parents alone must take responsibility for what their children watch.

Supporters of the proposal, however, point out that children's shows have turned into half-hour commercials. They insist that government regulation is necessary to protect children from the blatant exploitation of commercialism. They demand that children's programming respect the special needs and relative immaturity of the young, rather than manipulate them for profit.

The structure of the two positions is outlined here for you:

CONCLUSION: *The government should not regulate children's television programming.*

REASON: *Parents should be the source of any such regulation.*

CONCLUSION: *The government should regulate children's programming.*

REASON: *Children are especially vulnerable to exploitation by those wishing to profit from television programming.*

Notice that the opposition reasons that regulation is undesirable because it infringes on the individual parent's responsibility to monitor television viewing. They believe that it is up to the individual to decide what is and is not desirable. Thus, government regulation interferes with individuals' responsibility for monitoring what happens in their own homes.

VALUE ASSUMPTION: *In this context, individual responsibility is more important than collective responsibility.*

On the other hand, supporters of the proposal insist that help from the government is necessary for the greater good of the nation's children. They believe that a reduction in the exploitation of children is worth a minor cutback in individual responsibility. They think that the collective action of the government can more effectively reduce exploitation than is likely from the efforts of individuals.

VALUE ASSUMPTION: *In this situation, collective responsibility is more important than personal responsibility.*

Therefore, the major value conflict is collective responsibility versus individual responsibility. A supporter of the proposal makes the value assumption that collective responsibility in the form of government intervention is more important than unchecked individual responsibility. Her stance on this issue does not mean that she does not value individual responsibility; both values are probably very important to her. In this case, however, collective responsibility has taken priority. Similarly, opponents of the proposal do not advocate the exploitation of children. In this case, they believe that the preservation of individual responsibility takes precedence over collective action.

Remember that complete reasoning with respect to prescriptive issues requires reasons *and* value assumptions.

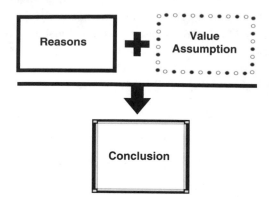

Let's complete one more example together.

Students should obey a dress code that includes uniforms, shoe restrictions, and hair length. In such an educational setting, teachers can teach and students can learn. Valuable time and energy will not be wasted on the discipline problems that arise in the absence of a rigid dress code.

Let's first outline the structure of the argument.

CONCLUSION: *Students should obey a rigid dress code.*

REASON: *Discipline problems would be reduced as a result of obedience to such a code.*

What value assumption do you think would result in someone's support for a rigid dress code for the schools? Look back at the table on page 60. Would any of the sample value conflicts affect one's reaction to school dress codes and the use of the above reasoning? Try to explain how a preference for educational excellence over individual self-expression might affect your reaction to this controversy.

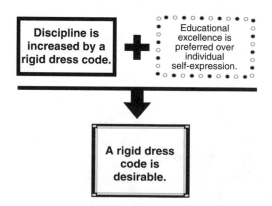

# USING THIS CRITICAL QUESTION

Once you have found a value assumption, what do you do with it? First, recall the purpose of every critical question—to move you toward the evaluation of reasoning! Because you know that thoughtful people have different value assumptions, you have the right to wonder why any single value assumption is being made. Thus, as a critical thinker, you would want to point out the need for anyone who is making an argument to offer some explanation for why you should accept the particular value assumption that is implicit in that argument.

## Values and Relativism

We do not want to give the impression in this chapter that value preferences are like ice cream, such that when I choose blueberry cheesecake as my flavor, you have no basis for trying to persuade me that the lemon chiffon is a better choice. Ice cream is just a matter of personal preference—end of story!

However, the choice of value preferences requires reasoning. That reasoning, like any other, can be informed, thoughtful, and caring. But it can also be sloppy and self-absorbed to some degree. Hence, value preferences require some justification that critical thinkers can consider. The Web site to be used in connection with this book (http://www.prenhall.com/browne) presents some of the classical avenues that people have used to substantiate their value assumptions. Please consider those options and inquire of people making a value judgment what basis they are providing for their preference.

## Summary

Assumptions are unstated ideas, taken for granted in the reasoning. Within the context of social controversies, they will consist of a preference for one value over another in a particular context. The author's background, reaction to projected consequences of acting on a particular value assumption, analogous controversies, and reverse role-playing all provide possible clues for finding a person's value assumptions in a particular controversy.

## Practice Exercises

[?]  *Critical Question:* **What are the value conflicts and assumptions?**

Identify the value conflicts that could lead to agreement or disagreement with the following points of view, then identify the value priorities assumed by the writer.

Passage 1

I would not like to see women in combat. If a war breaks out, all of us want only the most qualified people to be fighting for our country. I fear that women would not be able to handle the emotional strains involved in battle. Their strength as humans is in caring and nurturing. Let's let them do what they can do best.

And, just to show that I have no gender bias against women, I want to point out that men are too weak to fight when women are present. They would be distracted by the desire to protect their female comrades. Men are weak in this regard. In conclusion, the needs of women, men, and our country in general speak against permitting women to go into combat.

Passage 2

For most people, college is a waste of time and money. One does not need schools to learn. If you go to college to make it possible to earn more money, you have been had. More than half of those who earn more than $35,000 never received a college diploma. What you do learn in college is rarely useful on the job. Most of you would be better off saving part of the money you earn while your naive friends are in college.

Passage 3

Brazil is one of the few countries that possess precious rainforests. It is also a poor country relying on the destruction of the rainforest to supply much of its income. Brazilians use the rainforest to make products to fuel industrialized nations' craving for comfortable living and "all natural" products.

What we need to do in industrialized nations is raise tariffs drastically on rainforest products not only from Brazil but also from all countries that destroy rainforests. The entire world needs to recognize the rapid dwindling of this precious ecosystem, and tariffs are the tool to give a wake-up call to these equatorial countries. Tariffs would make it cost more to produce and sell rainforest products and ultimately make it less and less attractive to do business in these ecosystems.

## Sample Responses

Passage 1

CONCLUSION: *Women should not be permitted in combat situations.*

REASONS:   1. *They lack the necessary emotional toughness.*
2. *Their comparative strength lies elsewhere, for example, in nurturing and caring.*
3. *Men are so weak that they would be unable to fight well if women were in combat, because they would feel the need to protect female soldiers.*

One value conflict that relates to this argument is between tradition and equality of opportunity. Women have not traditionally been in combat situations in our country. Yet, we know that some women seek this opportunity. Men have it; the women applicants quite understandably say, "What about us?" The author makes the standard traditional arguments against using women in combat: They aren't up to it; they do a greater service at home; and they provide a dangerous distraction to our male troops on the battlefield. A value preference for tradition over equality of opportunity links the reasons to the conclusion.

As with most prescriptive controversies, more than one value conflict is involved in this dilemma. For example, this controversy also requires us to think about the rights of the individual versus the welfare of the community, as well as the tension between ambition and comfort.

Passage 2

CONCLUSION: *Most young people should not attend college.*

REASONS:   1. *Many of those who make a lot of money never attended college.*
           2. *College does not generally teach job-related skills.*

A value assumption is that materialistic achievement is more important than wisdom. Notice that the consequences stressed by the author is the impact of college on future income. She addresses none of the other purposes one might have for attending college. If one valued wisdom more than monetary accumulation, one might well reject the reasoning suggested in this passage.

 **CRITICAL QUESTION SUMMARY: WHY THIS QUESTION IS IMPORTANT**

### What Are the Value Conflicts and Assumptions?

While an author usually offers explicit reasons why she comes to a certain conclusion, she also makes certain assumptions that lead her to a certain conclusion. By identifying value conflicts, you determine whether the author's value preferences match your value preferences. Consequently, you have a tool for determining whether you will accept or reject an author's conclusion.

# 6

# WHAT ARE THE DESCRIPTIVE ASSUMPTIONS?

You should now be able to identify value assumptions—very important hidden links in prescriptive arguments. When you find value assumptions, you know pretty well what a writer or speaker wants the world to be like—what ideals he thinks are most important to seek. But you do not know what he takes for granted about what the world was, is, or will be like. His visible reasoning depends on these ideas, as well as upon his values. Such unstated ideas are descriptive assumptions, and they are essential hidden links in an argument.

A brief argument concerning Professor Starr depends on such hidden assumptions. Can you find them?

> You will learn a lot from Professor Starr. His students all rave about his lectures.

This chapter focuses on the identification of descriptive assumptions.

(?) *Critical Question:* **What are the descriptive assumptions?**

*Descriptive assumptions* are beliefs about the way the world is; prescriptive or value assumptions, you remember, are beliefs about how the world should be.

## Illustrating Descriptive Assumptions

Let's examine our argument about Professor Starr more closely to illustrate more clearly what we mean by a descriptive assumption.

The reasoning structure is:

> CONCLUSION: *You will learn a lot from Professor Starr.*
>
> REASON: *His students all rave about his lectures.*

The reasoning thus far is incomplete. We know that, *by itself,* a reason cannot support a conclusion; the reason must be connected to the conclusion by certain other (frequently unstated) ideas. These ideas are ones, which if true, justify treating the reason as support for the conclusion. Thus, whether a reason supports, or is relevant to, a conclusion depends on whether we can locate unstated ideas that logically connect the reason to the conclusion. When such unstated ideas are descriptive, we call them *descriptive assumptions.* Let us present two such assumptions for the above argument.

> ASSUMPTION 1: *Students' rave reviews are a good indicator of how much is learned from a lecture.*

First, note that if the reason is true and if this assumption is true, then the reason provides some support for the conclusion. If students, however, rave about lectures because of their entertainment value rather than because of their contribution to wisdom, then the reason given is not supportive of the conclusion. Next, note that this assumption is a statement about the way things are, not about the way things *should be.* Thus, it is a *descriptive connecting assumption.*

> ASSUMPTION 2: *To learn a lot means to absorb material from a lecture.*

(Sponge model thinking, right?) If "learn a lot" is defined as developing thinking skills, then the amount of raving about lectures may be irrelevant. Thus, this conclusion is supported by the reason only if a certain definition of learning is assumed.

We can call this kind of descriptive assumption a *definitional assumption* because we have taken for granted one meaning of a term that could have more than one meaning. Thus, one important kind of descriptive assumption to look for is a *definitional assumption*—the taking for granted of one meaning for a term that has multiple possible meanings. Let's see what this process looks like in argument form:

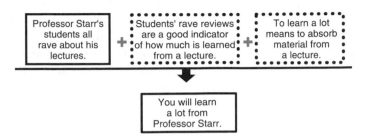

Once you have identified the connecting assumptions, you have answered the question, "On what basis can that conclusion be drawn from that reason?" The next natural step is to ask, "Is there any basis for accepting the assumptions?" If not, then, for you, the reason fails to provide support for the conclusion. If so, then the reason provides logical support for the conclusion. Thus, you can say reasoning is sound when you have identified connecting assumptions and you have good reason to believe those assumptions.

> **Attention:**   A descriptive assumption is an unstated belief about how the world is, or will become.

Note that there are further hidden assumptions in the above argument. For example, you should not be convinced by this reasoning unless you believe that the qualities others look for in lectures are the same qualities you look for. Should you eat at a restaurant because many of your friends rave about it? Wouldn't you want to know *why* they rave about it? *Remember:* Reasoning will usually contain multiple assumptions.

Note also that when you identify assumptions, you identify ideas the communicator *needs* to take for granted for the reason to be supportive of the conclusion. Because writers and speakers frequently are not aware of their own assumptions, their conscious beliefs may be quite different from the ideas you identify as implicit assumptions. When you then make the hidden connecting tissue of an argument visible, you also contribute to their understanding of their own argument and may thereby guide them to better beliefs and decisions.

## USING THIS CRITICAL QUESTION

After you have found descriptive assumptions, you want to think about whether there is a strong basis for accepting them. It is certainly fair for you to expect the person making the argument to provide you with some justification for why you should accept these particular assumptions. Finally, if the assumption is not supported and you find it questionable, you are behaving responsibly when you decide not to buy the argument. Your point in rejecting it is not to disagree with the conclusion. Instead, you are saying that you cannot accept the conclusion *based on the reasons offered so far.*

## Clues for Locating Assumptions

Your job in finding assumptions is to reconstruct the reasoning by filling in the missing gaps. That is, you want to provide ideas that help the communicator's reasoning "make sense." Once you have a picture of the entire argument, both the visible and the invisible parts, you will be in a much better position to determine its strengths and weaknesses.

How does one go about finding these important missing links? It requires hard work, imagination, and creativity. Finding important assumptions is a difficult task.

You have been introduced to two types of assumptions—value assumptions and descriptive assumptions. In the previous chapter, we gave you several hints for finding value assumptions. Here are some clues that will make your search for descriptive assumptions successful.

**Keep thinking about the gap between the conclusion and reasons.**   Why are you looking for assumptions in the first place? You are looking because you want to be able to judge how well the reasons support the conclusions. Thus, look for what the writer or speaker would have had to take for granted to link the reasons and conclusion. Keep asking, *"How do you get from the reason to the conclusion?"* Ask, *"If the reason is true, what else must be true for the conclusion to follow?"* And, to help answer that question, you will find it very helpful to ask, *"Supposing the reason(s) were true, is there any way in which the conclusion nevertheless could be false?"*

Searching for the gap will be helpful for finding both value and descriptive assumptions.

**Look for ideas that support reasons.**   Sometimes a reason is presented with no explicit support; yet the plausibility of the reason depends on the acceptability of ideas that have been taken for granted. These ideas are descriptive assumptions. The following brief argument illustrates such a case:

CONCLUSION: *We need to increase the money spent on AIDS education.*

REASON: *If we do so, it will greatly reduce the number of cases of AIDS.*

What ideas must be taken for granted for this reason to be acceptable? We must assume:

(a) the money will be spent in an effective manner; in other words, the education will reach members of high-risk groups that are not already being reached, and

(b) such members will be willing and able to respond to the educational message.

Thus, both (a) and (b) are ideas that have to be taken for granted for the reasons to be acceptable and, thus, supportive of the conclusion.

**Identify with the writer or speaker.**   Locating someone's assumptions is often made easier by imagining that you were asked to defend the conclusion. If you can, crawl into the skin of a person who would reach such a conclusion. Discover his background. Whether the person whose conclusion you are evaluating is a corporate executive, a labor leader, a boxing promoter, or a judge, try to play the role of such a person and plan in your mind what he would be thinking as he moves toward the conclusion. When an executive for a coal company argues that strip mining does not significantly harm the beauty of our natural environment, he has probably begun with a belief that strip mining is beneficial to our nation. Thus, he may assume a definition of beauty that would be consistent with his arguments, while other definitions of beauty would lead to a condemnation of strip mining.

**Identify with the opposition.**   If you are unable to locate assumptions by taking the role of the speaker or writer, try to reverse roles. Ask yourself why anyone might disagree with the conclusion. What type of reasoning would prompt someone to disagree with the conclusion you are evaluating? If you can play the role of a person who would not accept the conclusion, you can more readily see assumptions in the explicit structure of the argument.

**Recognize the potential existence of other means of attaining the advantages referred to in the reasons.**   Frequently, a conclusion is supported by reasons that indicate the various advantages of acting on the author's conclusion.

When there are many ways to reach the same advantages, one important assumption linking the reasons to the conclusion is that the best way to attain the advantages is through the one advocated by the communicator.

Let's try this technique with one brief example. Many counselors would argue that a college freshman should be allowed to choose her own courses without any restrictions from parents or college personnel because it facilitates the growth of personal responsibility. But aren't there many ways to encourage the growth of personal responsibility? Might not some of these alternatives have less serious disadvantages than those that could result when a freshman makes erroneous judgments about which courses would be in her best long-term interest? For example, requiring a student to make a substantial financial contribution to the cost of her education advances the development of personal responsibility. Thus, those who argue that it is desirable to permit college freshman to make their own course choices because such an opportunity encourages personal responsibility are assuming that there are not any less risky alternatives for accomplishing a similar goal.

**Avoid stating incompletely established reasons as assumptions.**   When you first attempt to locate assumptions you may find yourself locating a stated reason, thinking that the reason has not been adequately established, and asserting, "That's only an assumption. You don't know that to be the case." Or you might simply restate the reason as the assumption. You may have correctly identified a need on the part of the writer or speaker to better establish the truth of his reason. While this clarification is an important insight on your part, you have not identified an assumption in the sense that we have been using it in these two chapters. You are simply labeling a reason "an assumption."

Here is an example of stating an incompletely established reason as an assumption.

> High salaries are ruining professional sports, and a major reason is that the high salaries are alienating fans.

Now, challenge the argument by identifying the following assumption: The writer is assuming that high salaries really are alienating fans.

Do you see that when you do this, all you are doing is stating that the author's reason is her assumption—when what you are probably really trying to stress is that the author's reason has not been sufficiently established by evidence.

## Applying the Clues

Let's look at an argument about the impact of rock music and see whether we can identify descriptive and value assumptions.

> The immense attraction of rock music for college students is having a negative impact on their scholarship. Books no longer claim the enthusiasm that is now directed to the rock star of the week. How can we expect students to struggle with a lengthy passage from Plato when they have become accustomed to experiencing the throbbing, pulsating, primitive excitement of rock music? Such music provides premature ecstasy—like a drug—an instant ecstasy that books and the classroom cannot provide them. Furthermore, with the prevalence of the portable CD player, students can be constantly plugged into music. With so much time devoted to music (the hour spent in line for concert tickets, the concerts themselves, not to mention listening time alone), studies must suffer.
>
> Not only is rock music competing for our students' attention, but, increasingly, students are turning to rock for answers to both personal and universal problems. The socially conscious rock star is the new hero of the young. The solutions offered by such rock stars, however, are guilty of oversimplification. The weighty problems of the day cannot be adequately addressed in a five-minute lyric. Nevertheless, students are absorbing the words of millionaire musicians with far more reverence than they display toward their lessons or professors.
>
> CONCLUSION: *Rock music is having a negative impact on college learning.*
>
> REASONS:  1. *Books require much contemplative effort; thus, they can't compete with the easy, instant gratification provided by rock music.*
> 2. *Attention directed to rock music diverts attention from studies.*
> 3. *Students are absorbing the oversimplified messages of the music rather than the complex ideas of their professors.*

First, note that the author provides no "proof" for her reasons. Thus, you might be tempted to state, "Those reasons are only assumptions; she does not know that." Wrong! They are not *assumptions! Remember:* identifying less-than-fully established reasons, though important, is not the same as identifying assumptions—ideas that are taken for granted as a basic part of the argument.

Now, let's see whether any descriptive assumptions can be found in the argument. Remember to keep thinking about the gap between the conclusion and the reasons as you look. First, ask yourself, "Is there any basis for believing that the reason(s) might not be true?" Then ask, "Supposing the reason(s) were true, is there any way in which the conclusion nevertheless could be false?" Try to play the role of a person who is strongly attracted to rock music.

Look at the first two reasons. Neither would be true if it were the case that excitement of the passions and excitement of the intellect can work in harmony rather than in disharmony. Perhaps listening to rock music reduces tension for students such that they are less distracted when they are engaged in intellectual effort. Thus, one descriptive assumption is that *listening to rock music does not provide a relaxation effect.* Also, for the second reason to be true, it would have to be the case that *the time used for rock music is time that would otherwise be devoted to scholarly effort* (descriptive assumption). Perhaps the time devoted to rock music is "surplus time" for students.

Let's now suppose that the first two reasons were true. Rock music still might not have a negative impact on learning if it is the case that students are so motivated to learn that they will make an effort to overcome any potential negative effects. Thus, an assumption connecting the first two reasons to the conclusion is that *students are not sufficiently motivated to learn to overcome the obstacles posed by rock music's attraction.* Another connecting assumption is that *those who listen often to rock music are the same students who would be interested in scholarly activity.*

Consider the third reason. It is true only if it is the case that students process the messages of rock music just as they might process book and classroom messages. Perhaps the messages are processed as "entertainment," in the way a rollercoaster ride is processed. Thus, an important assumption is that *students fail to discriminate between messages provided by rock music and those provided by the classroom.*

Note also that there is a prescriptive quality to this essay; thus, important value assumptions underlie the reasoning. What is the author concerned about preserving? Try reverse role-playing. What would someone who disagreed with this position care about? What are the advantages to young people of listening to rock music? Your answers to these questions should lead you to the essay's value preference. For example, can you see how a preference for the cultivation of the intellect over gratification of the senses links the reasons to the conclusion?

## Avoiding Analysis of Trivial Assumptions

Writers and speakers take for granted certain self-evident things about which we should not concern ourselves. You will want to devote your energy to evaluating important assumptions, so we want to warn you about some potential trivial assumptions.

You as a reader or listener can assume that the communicator believes his reasons are true. You may want to attack the reasons as insufficient, but it is trivial to point out the writer's or speaker's assumption that the reasons are true.

Another type of trivial assumption concerns the reasoning structure. You may be tempted to state that the writer believes that the reason and conclusion are logically related. Right—but trivial. What is important is how they are logically related. It is also trivial to point out that an argument assumes that we can understand the logic, that we can understand the terminology, or that we have the appropriate background knowledge.

Avoid spending time on analyzing trivial assumptions. Your search for assumptions will be most rewarding when you locate hidden, debatable missing links.

## Assumptions and Your Own Writing and Speaking

When you attempt to communicate with an audience, either by writing or speaking, you will be making numerous assumptions. Communication requires them. But, once again out of respect for your audience, you should acknowledge those assumptions, and, where possible, provide a rationale for why you are making those particular assumptions.

The logic of this approach on your part is to assist the audience in accepting your argument. You are being open and fair with them. An audience should appreciate your willingness to present your argument in its fullness.

## Summary

Assumptions are ideas that, if true, enable us to claim that particular reasons provide support for a conclusion.

---

### Clues for Discovering Descriptive Assumptions

1. Keep thinking about the gap between the conclusion and reasons.
2. Look for ideas that support reasons.
3. Identify with the opposition.
4. Recognize the potential existence of other means of attaining the advantages referred to in the reasons.
5. Learn more about the issues.

---

## Practice Exercises

 *Critical Question:* **What are the descriptive assumptions?**

For each of the three passages, locate important assumptions made by the author. Remember first to determine the conclusion and the reasons.

Passage 1

Should it be legal for newspaper and television reporters to refuse to reveal their confidential sources? Indeed it should. The reporter-informant relationship is, after all, similar to those of priest and penitent, lawyer and client, physician and patient—all of which have a degree of privacy under the law. Moreover, if that relationship were not protected, the sources of information needed by the public would dry up.

Passage 2

Critical-thinking programs will not work. Critical-thinking skills should be taught like all other bodily skills, by coaching, not by combining lectures with textbooks that claim to teach people specific thinking skills. After all, we don't teach doctors and lawyers how to think critically by giving them a course in critical thinking. We require them to **use** critical-thinking skills in all courses that they are taught. We teach them by coaching, by providing lots of practice and corrective feedback.

Thinking is not a skill that can be taught in isolation from other mental acts and from the content of our disciplines. Instead of developing critical-thinking programs, we should be making sure that our students are coached in critical thinking in all their courses. If all our teachers would act as coaches and require our students to think about what is being taught instead of having them memorize the facts, then we would not need critical-thinking courses.

Passage 3

Values should not be taught in public schools. Teachers are not trained theologians, and such teaching results in the illegal union of church and state.

Second, it would be extremely insensitive towards students of a minority religion. School should be the place for the exploration of new ideas and sensitivity towards these ideas.

Anyway, teachers are not necessarily the best choices for value educators. They are merely adults who went to college and have no special moral understanding.

## Sample Responses

In presenting assumptions for the following arguments, we will list only some of the assumptions being made—those which we believe are among the most significant.

Passage 1

CONCLUSION: *It should be legal for newspaper and television reporters to refuse to reveal their confidential sources.*

REASONS:    1. *The reporter-informant relationship is special.*
           2. *If the relationship is not protected, sources of information will dry up.*

The author compares the reporter-informant relationship to others. The first reason will be less acceptable if the reasons for privacy of lawyer and client or physician and patient are quite different from what they are for the reporter-informant relationship. For example, reporters, unlike these other professionals, regularly make their information public, creating a number of social consequences for individuals in society.

A major assumption necessary for the second reason to be acceptable is that most of the information reporters rely on for their stories comes from sources who would be so severely frightened by the threat of being revealed that they would refuse to provide information. It may be the case that many individuals would still come forth to provide information because they could tolerate the risk.

Passage 2

CONCLUSION: *Critical-thinking programs will not work. Instead, we should make sure that students are coached in critical thinking in all of their courses.*

REASON: *Such skills can be better taught by coaching students within their respective disciplines.*

(SUPPORTING REASONS)

a.    *Lawyers and physicians are taught by coaching, not by critical-thinking courses.*
b.    *Thinking cannot be taught apart from the content of a discipline.*

Try reverse role-playing, taking the position of someone who teaches a critical-thinking course, perhaps using *Asking the Right Questions.*

For the reason to be true, it must be the case that most discipline-centered courses include, or are likely to include, the coaching of critical-thinking skills as an important part of the course. This assumption may be a form of wishful thinking. Much research suggests that most courses do not coach critical-thinking skills, but instead rely on lecturing and the reproduction of knowledge, and that most teachers may be very reluctant to change that emphasis.

Does the first supporting reason support the major reason? It does if the procedures used to train lawyers and physicians to think are successful and the training of lawyers and physicians is typical of the teaching in all disciplines. Perhaps these professionals could benefit greatly from a critical-thinking course that focuses on basic skills.

An important link between the reason and the conclusion is the assumption that it is not helpful to later coaching to have a good grounding in the basic skills. Coaching might be most successful in cases in which the learner has been explicitly taught the basic skills at an earlier time.

## CRITICAL QUESTION SUMMARY: WHY THIS QUESTION IS IMPORTANT

### What Are the Descriptive Assumptions?

When you identify descriptive assumptions, you are identifying the link between a reason and the author's conclusion. If this link is flawed, the reason does not necessarily lead to the conclusion. Consequently, identifying the descriptive assumptions allows you to determine whether an author's reasons lead to a conclusion. You will want to accept a conclusion only when there are good reasons that lead to the conclusion. Thus, when you determine that the link between the reasons and conclusion is flawed, you will want to be reluctant to accept the author's conclusion.

# ARE THERE ANY FALLACIES IN THE REASONING?

Thus far, you have been working at taking the raw materials a writer or speaker gives you and assembling them into a meaningful overall structure. You have learned ways to remove the irrelevant parts from your pan as well as how to discover the "invisible glue" that holds the relevant parts together—that is, the assumptions. All these things have been achieved by asking critical questions. Let's briefly review these questions:

1. What are the issue and the conclusion?
2. What are the reasons?
3. What words or phrases are ambiguous?
4. What are the value conflicts and assumptions?
5. What are the descriptive assumptions?

Asking these questions should give you a clear understanding of the communicator's reasoning as well as a sense of where there might be strengths and weaknesses in the argument. Most remaining chapters focus on how well the structure holds up after being assembled. Your major question now is, "How acceptable is the conclusion in light of the reasons provided?" You are now ready to make your central focus *evaluation*. *Remember:* The objective of critical reading and listening is to judge the acceptability or worth of conclusions.

While answering our first five questions has been a necessary beginning to the evaluation process, we now move to questions requiring us to make judgments more directly and explicitly about the worth or the quality of the reasoning. Our task now is to separate the "fools gold" from the genuine gold. We want to isolate the best reasons—those that we want to treat most seriously.

Your first step at this stage of the evaluation process is to examine the reasoning structure to determine whether the communicator has used a questionable assumption or has "tricked" you through either a mistake in logic or other forms of deceptive reasoning. Chapter 6 focused on finding and then thinking about the quality of assumptions. This chapter, on the other hand, highlights those reasoning "tricks" that we and others call *fallacies*.

Three common tricks are the following:

1. providing reasoning that requires *erroneous or incorrect assumptions,*
2. *distracting us* by making information seem relevant to the conclusion when it is not,
3. providing support for the conclusion that depends on the conclusion's already being true.

Spotting such tricks will prevent us from being unduly influenced by them. Let's see what a fallacy in reasoning looks like.

> Dear Editor: I was shocked by your paper's support of Senator Spendall's arguments for a tax hike to increase state money available for improving highways. Of course the Senator favors such a hike. What else would you expect from a tax and spend liberal!

Note that the letter at first appears to be presenting a "reason" to dispute the tax hike proposal, by citing the senator's liberal reputation. But the reason is *not relevant* to the conclusion. The question is whether the tax hike is a good idea. The letter writer has ignored the senator's reasons and has provided no specific reasons against the tax hike; instead, he has personally attacked the senator. In addition, the use of the *name-calling* phrase "tax and spend liberal" *appeals to the reader's emotions,* distracting us from the basic issue. The writer has committed a fallacy in reasoning—an ad hominem argument and, as with many fallacies, the name-calling is an illegitimate appeal to the reader's emotions.

This chapter gives you practice in identifying such fallacies.

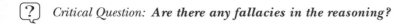 Critical Question: **Are there any fallacies in the reasoning?**

**Attention:** A fallacy is a reasoning "trick" that an author might use while trying to persuade you to accept a conclusion.

## A Questioning Approach to Finding Reasoning Fallacies

There are numerous reasoning fallacies, and they can be organized in many different ways. Many are so common that they have been given formal names. You can find many lengthy lists of fallacies in numerous texts and Web sites. Fortunately, it is not necessary for you to be aware of all the common fallacies and their names to be able to locate them. If you ask yourself the right questions, you will be able to find reasoning fallacies—even if you can't name them.

Thus, we have adopted the strategy of emphasizing self-questioning strategies, rather than asking you to memorize an extensive list of possible kinds of fallacies. We believe, however, that knowing the names of the most common fallacies can sensitize you to fallacies and also act as a language "shortcut" in communicating your reaction to faulty reasoning to others familiar with the names. So we provide you with the names of fallacies as we identify the deceptive reasoning processes and encourage you to learn the names of the common fallacies listed on page 98 at the end of the chapter.

We have already identified one fallacy for you in the previous section: Ad hominem arguments. You can start your list of fallacy names with this one. Here is its definition:

---

F: **Ad hominem:**   An attack, or an insult, on the person, rather than directly addressing the person's reasons.

---

## Evaluating Assumptions as a Starting Point

If you have been able to locate assumptions (see Chapters 5 and 6), especially descriptive assumptions, you already possess a major skill in determining questionable assumptions and in finding fallacies. The more questionable the assumption, the less relevant the reasoning. Some "reasons" will be so ir-relevant to the conclusion that you would have to supply blatantly erroneous assumptions to provide a logical link. Such reasoning is a fallacy, and you should immediately reject it.

In the next section, we take you through some exercises in discovering other common fallacies. Once you know how to look, you will be able to find most fallacies. We suggest that you adopt the following thinking steps in locating fallacies:

1. Identify the conclusions and reasons.

2. Always keep the conclusion in mind and consider reasons that you think might be relevant to it; contrast these reasons with the author's reasons.

3. Determine whether the reason states a specific and/or concrete advantage or a disadvantage; if not, be wary!

4. Identify any necessary assumption by asking yourself, "If the reason were true, what would one have to believe for it to logically support the conclusion, and does one have to believe for the reason to be true?"

5. Ask yourself, "Do these assumptions make sense?" If an obviously erroneous assumption is being made, you have found a fallacy in reasoning; and that reasoning can then be rejected.

6. Check the possibility of being distracted from relevant reasons by phrases that strongly appeal to your emotions.

To demonstrate the process you should go through to evaluate assumptions and thus recognize many fallacies, we will examine the quality of the reasoning in the following passage. We will begin by assembling the structure.

> The question involved in this legislation is not really a question of whether al-cohol consumption is or is not detrimental to health. Rather, it is a question of whether Congress is willing to have the Federal Communications Commission (FCC) make an arbitrary decision that prohibits alcohol advertising on radio and television. If we should permit the FCC to take this action in regard to al-cohol, what is there to prevent it from deciding next year that candy is detri-mental to the public health in that it causes obesity, tooth decay, and other health problems? What about milk and eggs? Milk and eggs are high in satu-rated animal fat and no doubt increase the cholesterol in the bloodstream, be-lieved by many heart specialists to be a contributing factor in heart disease. Do we want the FCC to be able to prohibit the advertising of milk, eggs, butter, and ice cream on TV?

Also, we all know that no action by the federal government, however drastic, can or will be effective in eliminating alcohol consumption completely. If people want to drink alcoholic beverages, they will find some way to do so.

CONCLUSION: *The FCC should not prohibit alcohol advertising on radio and television.*

REASONS:     1. *If we permit the FCC to prohibit advertising on radio and television, the FCC will soon prohibit many kinds of advertising, because many products present potential health hazards.*

2. *No action by the federal government can or will be effective in eliminating alcohol consumption completely.*

First, we should note that both reasons refer to rather specific disadvantages of the prohibition—a good start. The acceptability of the first reason, however, depends on a hidden assumption that once we allow actions to be taken on the merits of one case, it will be impossible to stop actions on similar cases. We do not agree with this assumption, because we believe that there are plenty of steps in our legal system to prevent such actions if they appear unjustified. Thus, we judge this reason to be unacceptable. Such reasoning is an example of the Slippery Slope fallacy.

---

F: **Slippery Slope:**     Making the assumption that a proposed step will set off an uncontrollable chain of undesirable events, when procedures exist to prevent such a chain of events.

---

The relevance of the second reason is questionable because even if this reason were true, the assumption linking the reason to the conclusion—the major goal of prohibiting alcohol advertising on radio and television is to *eliminate alcohol consumption completely*—is false. A more likely goal is to *reduce consumption.* Thus we reject this reason. We call this fallacy the Searching for Perfect Solutions fallacy. This fallacy takes the form: a solution to X does not deserve our support unless it destroys the problem entirely. If we ever find a perfect solution, then we should adopt it. But just because part of a problem would remain after a solution is tried does not mean the solution is unwise. A particular solution may be vastly superior to no solution at all. It may move us closer to solving the problem completely.

If we waited for perfect solutions to emerge, we would often find ourselves paralyzed, unable to act. Here is another example of this fallacy: Why try to restrict people's access to abortion clinics in the United States? Even if you were successful, a woman seeking an abortion could still fly to Europe to acquire an abortion.

---

**F: Searching for Perfect Solutions:**    Falsely assuming that because part of a problem would remain after a solution is tried, the solution should not be adopted.

---

## Discovering Other Common Reasoning Fallacies

We are now going to take you through some exercises in discovering more common fallacies. As you encounter each exercise, try to apply the fallacy-finding hints that we listed above. Once you have developed good fallacy detection habits, you will be able to find most fallacies. Each exercise presents some reasoning that includes fallacies. We indicate why we believe the reasoning is fallacious, then name and define the fallacy.

> Exercise A
>
> It's about time that we make marijuana an option for people in chronic severe pain. We approve drugs when society reaches a consensus about their value, and there is clearly now a consensus for such approval. A recent survey of public opinion reported that 73% thought medical marijuana should be allowed. In addition, the California Association for the Treatment of AIDS Victims supports smoking marijuana as a treatment option for AIDS patients. Anyone who would not support the legalization of medical marijuana has never sat for hours with someone crying out in pain and pleading to die just to stop the pain.

As a first step in analyzing for fallacies, let's outline the argument.

> CONCLUSION: *Smoking marijuana should be a medical option.*
>
> REASONS:    1. *We approve drugs when a consensus of their medical value has been reached, and a recent survey shows a consensus approving marijuana as a medical treatment.*
>             2. *A California association supports medical marijuana use.*
>             3. *Opponents of medical marijuana haven't been exposed to the pain of those in need.*

First, we should note that none of the reasons points out a specific advantage of medical marijuana; thus we should be wary from the start. Next, a close look at the wording in the first reason shows a shift in meaning of a key term, and this shift tricks us. The meaning of the word consensus shifts in such a way that it looks as if he has made a relevant argument when he has not. Consensus for drug approval usually means the consensus of scientific researchers about its merits, which is a very different consensus from the agreement of the American public on an opinion poll. Thus the reason fails to make sense, and we should reject it. We call this mistake in reasoning the Equivocation fallacy. Whenever you see a key word in an argument used more than once, check to see that the meaning has not changed; if it has, be alert to the Equivocation fallacy.

---

F: **Equivocation:**    A key word is used with two or more meanings in an argument such that the argument fails to make sense once the shifts in meaning are recognized.

---

Well, even if there is tricky use of the word *consensus,* don't the survey results by themselves still support the conclusion? Only if we accept the assumption that when something is popular, then it must be good—a mistaken assumption. The public often has not sufficiently studied a problem to provide a reasoned judgment. Be wary of appeals to common opinion, or to popular sentiment. We label this mistake in reasoning the Appeal to Popularity fallacy.

---

F: **Appeal to Popularity (Ad populum):**    An attempt to justify a claim by appealing to sentiments that large groups of people have in common; falsely assumes that anything favored by a large group is desirable.

---

Now, carefully examine the author's second reason. What assumption is being made? To prove that medical marijuana is desirable, he *appeals to questionable authorities—a California association.* A position is not good just because authorities are for it. What is important in determining the relevance of such reasoning is the evidence that the authorities are using in making their judgment. Unless we know that these authorities have special knowledge about this issue, we must treat this reason as a fallacy. Such a fallacy is called the Appeal to Questionable Authority fallacy.

**F: Appeal to Questionable Authority:**    Supporting a conclusion by citing an authority who lacks special expertise on the issue at hand.

Now let's examine some arguments related to another controversy: Should Congress approve a federally funded child-development program that would provide day-care centers for children?

Exercise B

I am against the government's child-development program. First, I am interested in protecting the children of this country. They need to be protected from social planners and *self-righteous ideologues* who would disrupt the normal course of life and tear them from their mothers and families to make them *pawns* in a universal scheme designed to produce infinite happiness in 20 years. Children should grow up with their mothers, not with a series of caretakers and nurses' aides. What is at issue is whether parents shall continue to have the right to form the characters of their children, or whether the State with all its power should be given the tools and techniques for forming the young.

Let's again begin by outlining the argument.

CONCLUSION:  *I am against the government's child-development program.*

REASONS:    1.  *Our children need to be protected from social planners and self-righteous ideologues, who would disrupt the normal course of life and tear them from their families.*
2.  *The parents, not the State, should have the right to form the characters of their children.*

As critical readers and listeners, we should be looking for specific facts about the program. Do you find any specifics in the first reason? No. The reason is saturated with undefined and emotionally loaded generalities. We have italicized several of these terms in the passage. Such terms will typically generate negative emotions, which the writer or speaker hopes readers and listeners will associate with the position she is attacking. Again, the writer is engaging in name-calling and emotional appeals. The use of emotionally charged negative terms serve to distract readers and listeners from the facts.

The writer has tricked us in another way. She states that the program will "tear them from their families and mothers," and the children will be "pawns in a universal scheme." Of course, nobody wants these things to happen to their children. However, the important question is whether in fact the bill will do these things. Not likely!

The writer is playing two common tricks on us. First, she is appealing to our emotions with her choice of words. Second, she has set up a position to attack which in fact does not exist, making it much easier to get us on her side. She has extended the opposition's position to an "easy-to-attack" position. The erroneous assumption in this case is that the position attacked is the same as the position actually presented in the legislation. The lesson for the critical thinker is: When someone attacks aspects of a position, always check to see whether she is fairly representing the position. If she is not, you have located the Straw Person fallacy.

A straw person is not real and is easy to knock down—as is the position attacked when someone commits the Straw Person fallacy. The best way to check how fairly a position is being represented is to get the facts about all positions.

---

F: **Straw Person:**    Distorting our opponent's point of view so that it is easy to attack; thus we attack a point of view that does not truly exist.

---

Let's now look closely at the second reason. The writer states that either parents have the right to form the characters of their children, or else the State should be given the decisive tools. For statements like this to be true, one must assume that there are only two choices. Are there? No! The writer has created a *false dilemma.* Isn't it possible for the child-development program to exist and also for the family to have a significant influence on the child? Always be cautious when controversies are treated as if only two choices are possible; there are frequently more than two. When a writer or speaker oversimplifies an issue by stating only two choices, the error is referred to as an Either-Or or False Dilemma fallacy. To find Either-Or fallacies, be on the alert for phrases like the following:

either . . . or

the only alternative is

the two choices are

because A has not worked, only B will

Seeing these phrases does not necessarily mean that you have located a fallacy. Sometimes there *are* only two options. These phrases are just caution signs causing you to pause and wonder: "But are there more than two options in this case?"

Can you see the false dilemma in the following interchange a few weeks after the September 11, 2001, terrorist attacks?

> Citizen: I think that the terrorist attacks have led to actions that have placed too many restrictions on our rights to privacy.
>
> Politician: Why do you hate America?

---

F: **Either-Or (False Dilemma):**    Assuming only two alternatives exist when it is possible that there are more than two.

---

The following argument contains another fallacy involving a mistaken assumption. Try to locate the assumption.

### Exercise C

> It doesn't make sense for you to give pop quizzes to your class, Professor Jones. It just makes a lot of extra work for you and makes the students nervous. Students should not need pop quizzes to motivate them to prepare for each class.

The advice to Professor Jones requires a faulty assumption to support the conclusion. That something *should* be true—students should not need pop quizzes to motivate them to prepare for class—in no way guarantees that what *is* true will conform to the prescription. Reality, or "what is," is often in conflict with "what should be."

Another common illustration of this reasoning error occurs when discussing proposals for government regulation. For instance, someone might argue that regulating advertising for children's television programs is undesirable because parents *should* change the channel or shut off the television if advertising is deceptive. Perhaps parents in a perfect world would behave in this fashion. Many parents, however, are too busy to monitor children's programming.

When reasoning requires us to assume that what we think *should be* matches *what is,* or *what will be,* it commits the Wishful Thinking fallacy. We would hope that what *should* be the case would guide our behavior. Yet many observations convince us that just because advertisers, politicians, and authors should not mislead us is no protection against their regularly misleading us. The world around us is a poor imitation of what the world should be like.

Here's a final example of wishful thinking that might sound familiar to you.

It can't be Thursday already; I haven't finished my paper yet.

---

F: **Wishful Thinking:**   Making the faulty assumption that because we wish X were true or false, then X is indeed true or false.

---

Another confusion is responsible for an error in reasoning that we often encounter when seeking explanations. To explain requires an analysis of why an event occurred. Explaining is demanding work that often tests the boundaries of what we know. When asked for an explanation, it's frequently tempting to hide our ignorance by labeling or naming what occurred. Then we assume that because we know the name, we know the cause.

We do so because the naming tricks us into believing we have identified something the person *has* or *is* that makes her act accordingly. For example, instead of specifying the complex set of internal and external factors that lead a person to manifest an angry emotion, such as parental reinforcement practices, lack of sleep, and life stressors, we say the person *has* a "bad temper," or that the person *is* hostile. Such explanations oversimplify and prevent us from seeking more insightful understanding.

The following examples should heighten your alertness to this fallacy:

1. In response to her father's heavy drinking, an adult daughter asks her mother, "Why is dad behaving so strangely?" Her mother replies, "He's *having* a midlife crisis."

2. A patient cries every time his counselor asks about his childhood. An intern who watched the counseling session asks the counselor, after the patient has left, "Why does he cry when you ask about his youth?" The counselor replies, "He's neurotic."

Neither respondent satisfactorily explained what happened. For instance, the specifics of dad's genes, job pressures, marital strife, and exercise habits could have provided the basis for explaining the heavy drinking. "A midlife crisis" is not only inadequate; it misleads. We think we know why dad is drinking heavily, but we don't.

Be alert for this error when people claim that they have discovered a cause for the behavior yet all they have done is named it.

---

F: **Explaining by Naming:**    Falsely assuming that because you have provided a name for some event or behavior that you have also adequately explained the event.

---

## Looking for Diversions

As you look for fallacies, you will find it helpful to be especially alert to reasoning used by the communicator that *diverts your attention* from the most relevant reasons. For example, the Name Calling and Ad hominem fallacies can trick us by diverting our attention too much to the nature of the person and too little to the legitimate reasons. In this section we present exercises that illustrate other fallacies that we are likely to detect if we ask the question: Has the author tricked us by diverting our attention?

> Exercise D
>
> Political speech: In the upcoming election, you have the opportunity to vote for a woman who represents the future of this great nation, who has fought for democracy and defended our flag, and who has been decisive, confident, and courageous in pursuing the American Dream. This is a caring woman who has supported our children and the environment and has helped move this country toward peace, prosperity, and freedom. A vote for Goodheart is a vote for truth, vision, and common sense.

Without our outlining the reasoning structure, you can see that the argument fails to provide any specifics about the senator's past record, but instead presents a series of *virtue words* that tend to be associated with deep-seated positive emotions. We call these virtue words "Glittering Generalities," because they have such positive associations and are so general as to mean whatever the reader wants them to mean. The Glittering Generality device leads us to approve or accept a conclusion without examining relevant reasons, evidence, or specific advantages or disadvantages. The Glittering Generality is much like name-calling in reverse, because name-calling seeks to make us form a negative judgment without examining the evidence. The use of virtue words is a popular ploy of politicians because it serves to distract the reader or listener from specific actions or policies, which can more easily trigger disagreement.

---

F: **Glittering Generality:**    The use of vague, emotionally appealing virtue words that dispose us to approve something without closely examining the reasons.

---

Let's examine another very common diversionary device.

Exercise E

I don't see how people can keep arguing that Japanese cars are a better buy than American cars. Why, just look at the recent performance of the Japanese economy compared to the American economy. They have experienced three years of economic decline, while we have enjoyed three years of relative prosperity.

What is the real issue? Which is a better car—Japanese or American? But if the reader is not careful, he will get involved instead in the question of how the two economies are doing. If so, the writer has diverted the reader's attention to another issue. When a writer or speaker redirects our attention from the issue, we can say that he has drawn a *red herring* across the trail of the argument. Many of us are adept at committing the Red Herring fallacy, as the following example illustrates:

If the daughter is successful, the issue will become whether the mother is picking on her daughter, not why the daughter was out late.

You should normally have no difficulty spotting red herrings as long as you keep the real issue in mind as well as the kind of evidence needed to resolve it.

F: **Red Herring:** An irrelevant topic is presented to divert attention from the original issue and help to "win" an argument by shifting attention away from the argument and to another issue. The fallacy sequence in this instance is as follows: (a) Topic A is being discussed; (b) Topic B is introduced as though it is relevant to Topic A, but it is not; (c) Topic A is abandoned.

This sort of "reasoning" is fallacious because merely changing the topic of discussion hardly counts as an argument against a claim.

## Sleight of Hand: Begging the Question

Our last illustrated fallacy is a particularly deceptive one. Sometimes a conclusion is supported by itself; only the words have been changed to fool the innocent! For example, to argue that dropping out of school is *undesirable* because it is *bad* is to argue not at all. The conclusion is "proven" by the conclusion (in different words). Such an argument *begs the question,* rather than answering it. Let's look at an example that is a little less obvious.

> Programmed-learning texts are clearly superior to traditional texts in learning effectiveness because it is highly advantageous for learning to have materials presented in a step-by-step fashion.

Again, the reason supporting the conclusion restates the conclusion in different words. By definition, programmed learning is a step-by-step procedure. The writer is arguing that such a procedure is good because it is good. A legitimate reason would be one that points out a specific advantage to programmed learning such as greater retention of learned material.

Whenever a conclusion is *assumed* in the reasoning when it should have been proven, begging the question has occurred. When you outline the structure of an argument, check the reasons to be sure that they do not simply repeat the conclusion in different words and check to see that the conclusion is not used to prove the reasons. In case you are confused, let's illustrate with two examples, one argument that begs the question and one that does not.

> (1) To allow the press to keep their sources confidential is very advantageous to the country because it increases the likelihood that individuals will report evidence against powerful people.

(2) To allow the press to keep their sources confidential is very advantageous to the country because it is highly conducive to the interests of the larger community that private individuals should have the privilege of providing information to the press without being identified.

Paragraph (2) begs the question by basically repeating the conclusion. It fails to point out what the specific advantages are, and simply repeats that confidentiality of sources is socially used.

---

F: **Begging the Question:**  An argument in which the conclusion is assumed in the reasoning.

---

## USING THIS CRITICAL QUESTION

When you spot a fallacy, you have found a legitimate basis for rejecting the argument. But in the spirit of constructive critical thinking, you want to continue the discussion of the issue. Unfortunately, the author of a book or article is unavailable for more conversation. But in those instances where the fallacy occurred in an oral argument, your best bet for an enduring conversation is to ask the person who committed the fallacy if there is not a better reason for the conclusion. For example, if a Red Herring fallacy occurs, ask the speaker if it would be possible to return to the original issue.

### Summary of Reasoning Errors

We have taken you through exercises that illustrate a number of ways in which reasoning may be erroneous. We have not listed all the ways, but we have given you a good start. We have saved some additional fallacies for later chapters because you are most likely to spot them when you focus on the particular question central to that chapter. As you encounter each additional fallacy, be sure to add it to your fallacy list.

To find reasoning fallacies, keep in mind what kinds of reasons are good reasons—that is, the evidence and the moral principles relevant to the issue. Reasoning should be *rejected* whenever you have found mistaken assumptions, distractions, or support for the conclusion that already assumes the truth of the conclusion. Reasoning should be *approached cautiously* when it appeals to group-approved attitudes and to authority. You should always ask, "Are there good reasons to consider such appeals as persuasive evidence?" A precautionary note is in order here: Do not automatically reject reasoning that relies on appeals to authority or group-approved attitudes. Carefully evaluate such reasoning. For example, if most physicians in the country choose to take up jogging, that information is important to consider in deciding whether jogging is beneficial. Some authorities do possess valuable information. Because of its importance as a source of evidence, we discuss appeals to authority in detail in the next chapter.

---

### Clues for Locating and Assessing Fallacies in Reasoning

**You should reject reasoning when the author:**

- attacks a person or a person's background, instead of the person's ideas
- uses slippery slope reasoning
- reflects a search for perfect solutions
- equivocates
- inappropriately appeals to common opinion
- appeals to questionable authority
- attacks a straw person
- presents a faulty dilemma
- engages in wishful thinking
- explains by naming
- diverts attention from the issue
- distracts with glittering generalities
- begs the question

---

## Expanding Your Knowledge of Fallacies

We recommend that you consult texts and some Web sites to expand your awareness and understanding of reasoning fallacies. Damer's *Attacking Faulty Reasoning* is a good source to help you become more familiar with reasoning fallacies. There are dozens of fallacy lists on the Web, which vary greatly in quality. A few of the more helpful sites, which provide descriptions and examples of numerous fallacies, are listed below:

The Nizkor Project: Fallacies
http://www.nizkor.org/features/fallacies/

The Fallacy Zoo by Brian Yoder (list of basic fallacies with examples)
http://www.primenet.com/~byoder/fallazoo.htm

The Fallacy Files by Gary Curtis
http://gncurtis.home.texas.net/index.html

Stephen's Guide to the Logical Fallacies
http://www.datanation.com/fallacies/

## Fallacies and Your Own Writing and Speaking

When you communicate, you necessarily engage in reasoning. If your purpose is to present a well-reasoned argument, in which you do not want to "trick" the reader into agreeing with you, then you will want to avoid committing reasoning fallacies. Awareness of possible errors committed by writers provides you with warnings to heed when you construct your own arguments. You can avoid fallacies by checking your own assumptions very carefully, by remembering that most controversial issues require you to get specific about advantages and disadvantages, and by keeping a checklist handy of possible reasoning fallacies.

## Practice Exercises

 Critical Question: **Are there any fallacies in the reasoning?**

Try to identify fallacies in the reasoning in each of the three practice passages.

Passage 1

The surgeon general has overstepped his bounds by recommending that explicit sex education begin as early as third grade. It is obvious that he is yet another victim of the AIDS hysteria sweeping the nation. Unfortunately, his media-influenced announcement has given new life to those who favor explicit sex education—even to the detriment of the nation's children.

Sexuality has always been a topic of conversation reserved for the family. Only recently has sex education been forced on young children. The surgeon general's recommendation removes the role of the family entirely. It should be up to parents to explain sex to their children in a manner with which they are comfortable. Sex education exclusive of the family is stripped of values or any sense of morality, and should thus be discouraged. For years families have taken the responsibility of sex education, and that's the way it should remain.

Sex education in schools encourages experimentation. Kids are curious. Letting them in on the secret of sex at such a young age will promote blatant promiscuity. Frank discussions of sex are embarrassing for children, and they destroy the natural modesty of girls.

### Passage 2

Sandra: I don't see why you are so against permitting beer to be sold at the new University Student Union. After all, a survey of our students shows that 80 percent are in favor of the proposal.

Joe: Of course, you would be in favor of serving any alcoholic beverage at any time, anywhere. You are one of the biggest alcoholics on our campus.

### Passage 3

Bill: Countries that harbor terrorists who want to destroy the United States must be considered enemies of the United States. Any country that does not relinquish terrorists to the American justice system is clearly on the side of the terrorists. This sort of action means that the leaders of these countries do not wish to see justice done to the terrorists and care more about hiding murderers, rapists, thieves, and anti-democrats.

Taylor: That's exactly the kind of argument that I would expect from someone who has relatives who have worked for the CIA. But it seems to me that once you start labeling countries that disagree with America on policy as enemies, then eventually almost all countries will be considered our enemies, and we will be left with no allies.

Bill: If that's the case, too bad. America stands for freedom, democracy, and truth. So it can stand against the world. Besides, the U.S. should be able to convince countries hostile to the United States of the error of their ways because our beliefs have a strong religious foundation.

Taylor: Do you really think most religious people are in favor of war? A Gallup poll last week found that 75 percent of highly religious people didn't think we should go to war with countries harboring terrorists.

Bill: I think that's an overestimate. How many people did they survey?

Taylor: I'm not sure. But getting back to your original issue, the biggest problem with a tough stand against countries that harbor terrorists is that such a policy is not going to wipe out terrorism in the world.

Bill: Why do you keep defending the terrorists? I thought you were a patriot. Besides, this is a democracy, and most Americans agree with me.

## Sample Responses

### Passage 1

CONCLUSION: *Sex education should not be taught in schools.*

REASONS:     1. *The Surgeon General's report reflects hysteria.*
2. *It is the job of parents.*
3. *Education encourages promiscuity.*

The author begins the argument by attacking the surgeon general rather than the issue. She claims that the recommendation is a by-product of the AIDS hysteria rather than extensive research. Her suggestion that the surgeon general issues reports in reaction to hot topics in the media undermines his credibility and character and is therefore *ad hominem.*

Her second reason confuses "what is" with "what should be." Just because sex education *should be* up to the parents does not mean that they *will* provide education.

The third reason presents a false dilemma—either keep sex education out of the schools or face morally loose, value-free children. But isn't it possible to have morally loose children even when sex education is taking place in the home? Isn't it also a possibility that both parents and the schools can play a role in sex education? Might not education result in children who are prepared to handle the issue of sex in their lives rather than morally deficient delinquents?

### Passage 2

SANDRA'S CONCLUSION:  *Beer should be served at the University Union.*

SANDRA'S REASON:  *Most students are in favor of the idea.*

JOE'S CONCLUSION:  *Beer should not be served in the University Union.* (implied)

JOE'S REASON:  *We should not listen to Sandra's argument because she is an alcoholic.*

Both Sandra and Joe commit fallacies in their arguments. Sandra bases her claim about the desirability of beer in the Union on the majority view of students that beer should be served. She makes the erroneous assumption that if the majority favors an action, the action is proper. Students might be for the proposal, but they also may have given little thought to the advantages and disadvantages of making beer more easily available.

Joe commits two fallacies in his tiny argument. First, he attacks Sandra, rather than addressing Sandra's reasoning. Sandra's alleged alcoholism is not the issue. She provides a reason for her support for beer in the Union; Joe ignores that reason and attacks her instead. Second, Joe responds to a Straw

Person argument when he responds to Sandra by extending what she did say to an extreme position that she did not take in her statement. Nowhere in her argument did Sandra favor drinking with no restrictions.

## CRITICAL QUESTION SUMMARY: WHY THIS QUESTION IS IMPORTANT

### Are There Any Fallacies in the Reasoning?

Once you have identified the reasons, you want to determine whether the author used any reasoning tricks, or fallacies. If you identify a fallacy in reasoning, that reason does not provide good support for the conclusion. Consequently, you would not want to accept an author's conclusion on the basis of that reason. If the author provides no good reasons, you would not want to accept his or her conclusion. Thus, looking for fallacies in reasoning is another important step in determining whether you will accept or reject the author's conclusion.

# 8

# How Good Is the Evidence: Intuition, Personal Experience, Testimonials, and Appeals to Authority?

In the last chapter you made major inroads into the process of evaluating persuasive communications by learning how to detect some fallacies in reasoning. In the following chapters, we continue our focus on evaluation as we learn to ask critical questions about a specific part of the reasoning structure: claims about the "facts." Let's see what such claims look like.

Eating oat bran reduces the risk of cancer.

Capital punishment deters crime.

College campuses are not safe; *Time* magazine reports that campus assaults have increased by 10 percent over the last three years.

What do we make of these claims? Are they legitimate? Most reasoning includes claims such as these. In this chapter, we begin the process of evaluating such claims.

[?] Critical Question: **How good is the evidence: intuition, personal experience, testimonials, and appeals to authority?**

## The Need for Evidence

Almost all reasoning we encounter includes beliefs about the way the world is, was, or is going to be that the communicator wants us to accept as "facts." These beliefs can be conclusions, reasons, or assumptions. We can refer to such beliefs as *factual claims.*

The first question you should ask about a factual claim is, *"Why should I believe it?"*

Your next question is, *"Does the claim need evidence to support it?"* If it does, and if there is no evidence, the claim is a *mere assertion.* You should seriously question the dependability of mere assertions!

If there is evidence, your next question is, *"How good is the evidence?"*

To evaluate reasoning, we need to remember that some factual claims can be counted on more than others. For example, you probably feel quite certain that the claim "most United States senators are men" is true, but less certain that the assertion "eating oat bran reduces the risk of heart attacks" is true.

Because it is extremely difficult, if not impossible, to establish the *absolute* truth or falsity of most claims, rather than ask whether they are *true*, we prefer to ask whether they are *dependable.* In essence, we want to ask, *"Can we count on such beliefs?"* The greater the quality and quantity of evidence supporting a claim, the more we can *depend on it*, and the more we can call the claim a *"fact."*

For example, abundant evidence exists that planes hijacked by terrorists crashed into the World Trade Center on September 11, 2001. Thus, we can treat that claim as a fact. On the other hand, there is much conflicting evidence for the belief "homosexuality is inherited." We thus can't treat this belief as a fact. The major difference between claims that are *opinions* and those that are *facts* is the present state of the relevant evidence. The more supporting evidence there is for a belief, the more "factual" the belief becomes.

Before we judge the persuasiveness of a communication, we need to know which factual claims are most dependable. How do we determine dependability? We ask questions like the following:

| | |
|---|---|
| What is your proof? | How do you know that's true? |
| Where's the evidence? | Why do you believe that? |
| Are you sure that's true? | Can you prove it? |

You will be well on your way to being among the best critical thinkers when you develop the habit of regularly asking these questions. They require those making arguments to be responsible by revealing the basis for their arguments. Anyone with an argument that you should consider will not hesitate to answer these questions. They know they have substantial support for their claims and, consequently, will want to share their evidence in the hope that you will learn to share their conclusions.

When we regularly ask these questions, we notice that for many beliefs there is insufficient evidence to clearly support or refute them. For example, much evidence supports the assertion that taking an aspirin every other day reduces the risk of heart attack, although some other evidence disputes it. In such cases, we need to make judgments about where the *preponderance of evidence* lies as we decide on the dependability of the factual claim.

Making such judgments requires us to ask the important question, *"How good is the evidence?"* The next three chapters focus on questions we need to ask to decide how well communicators have supported their factual claims. The more dependable the factual claims, the more persuasive the communications should be.

## Locating Factual Claims

We encounter factual claims as (a) *descriptive conclusions,* (b) *reasons* used to support either descriptive or prescriptive conclusions, or (c) as *descriptive assumptions.* Let's examine an example of each within brief arguments.

> (a) *Dieting may contribute to the development of eating disorders.* Researchers studied the dieting histories and the severity of binge-eating episodes among 111 women enrolled in a treatment program for eating disorders and found that 60 percent of the women reported that their first eating binge followed their initial dieting attempts.

Note that "dieting may contribute to the development of eating disorders" is a factual claim that is a descriptive conclusion supported by research evidence. In this case, we want to ask, "Is that conclusion—a factual claim—justified by the evidence?"

> (b) We should decrease the sizes of classes in our universities. *Large classes are leading to greater student alienation, according to recent government statistics.*

Note that the factual claim here is the generalization that "large classes are leading to greater student alienation," and it functions as a reason supporting a prescriptive conclusion. In this case, we want to ask, "Is that reason—a factual claim—justified by the evidence?"

> (c) We cannot afford any more immigrants in this country. The largest number of immigrants—over 6.5 million—have settled in California and cost California alone an estimated $3 billion annually in extra health care, schooling, and other public services. (Unstated descriptive assumption linking the reason to the conclusion: *The positive impact of immigrants on the economy, through such benefits as creating new jobs and paying taxes, is significantly less than the cost.*)

Note that this factual claim is a descriptive assumption, which may or may not be dependable. Before we believe the assumption, and thus the reason, we want to ask, "How well does evidence support the assumption?" You will find that while many communicators perceive the desirability of supporting their reasons with evidence, they don't see the need to make their assumptions explicit. Thus evidence for assumptions is rarely presented, even though in many cases such evidence would be quite helpful in deciding the quality of an argument.

## Sources of Evidence

When should we judge a factual claim as dependable? There are three instances in which we will be most inclined to agree with a factual claim:

1.   when the claim appears to be undisputed common knowledge, such as the claim "weight lifting increases muscular body mass."
2.   when the claim is the conclusion from a well-reasoned argument.
3.   when the claim is adequately supported by solid evidence in the same communication or by other evidence that we know.

Our concern in this chapter is the third instance. Determining the adequacy of evidence requires us to ask, "How good is the evidence?" To answer this question, we must first ask, "What do we mean by *evidence?*"

**Attention:**   Evidence is explicit information shared by the communicator that is used to back up or to justify the dependability of a factual claim (see Chapter 3). In prescriptive arguments, evidence will be needed to support reasons that are factual claims; in descriptive arguments, evidence will be needed to directly support a descriptive conclusion.

The quality of evidence depends on the kind of evidence it is. Thus, to evaluate evidence, we first need to ask, "What kind of evidence is it?" Knowing the kind of evidence tells us what questions we should ask.

Major kinds of evidence include:

- intuition
- personal experience
- testimonials
- appeals to authorities
- personal observations
- case examples
- research studies
- analogies

When used appropriately, each kind of evidence can be "good evidence." It can help support an author's claim. Like a gold prospector closely examining the gravel in his pan for potentially high-quality ore, we must closely examine the evidence to determine its quality. We want to know, "Does an author's evidence provide dependable support for her claim?" Thus, we begin to evaluate evidence by asking, *"How good is the evidence?"*

In this chapter and the next one, we examine what kinds of questions we can ask of each kind of evidence to help us decide. Kinds of evidence examined in this chapter are intuition, authority, and testimonials.

## Intuition as Evidence

When we use intuition to support a claim, we rely on "common sense," or on our "gut feelings," or on hunches. When a communicator supports a claim by saying "common sense tells us," or "I just know that it's true," he is using intuition as his evidence.

A major problem with intuition is that it is private; others have no way to judge its dependability. Thus, when intuitive beliefs differ, which is often the case, we have no solid basis for deciding which ones to believe. Also, much intuition relies on unconscious processing that largely ignores relevant evidence and reflects strong biases. Consequently, we must be very wary of claims backed up only by intuition.

However, sometimes "intuition" may in fact be relying on some other kind of evidence, such as extensive relevant personal experiences and readings. For example, when an experienced pilot has an intuition that the plane doesn't feel right as it taxis for takeoff, we might be quite supportive of further safety checks of the plane prior to takeoff. Sometimes "hunches" are not blind. As critical thinkers, we would want to find out whether claims relying on intuition have any other kinds of evidential support.

## Dangers of Appealing to Personal Experience as Evidence

The following arguments use a particular kind of evidence to support a factual claim.

> "I was placed in day care as a child, and I wasn't harmed by the experience. Thus I don't see any problems with putting children into day care."

> "I took anti-depressants for my depression and just got worse. I think drugs are being used too often to treat mental illness."

Both arguments appeal to personal experiences as evidence. Phrases like "I know someone who . . . ," and "In my experience, I've found . . ." should alert you to such evidence. Because personal experiences are very vivid in our memories, we often rely on them as evidence to support a belief. For example, you might have a really frustrating experience with a lawyer because she greatly overcharges you for her services, leading you to believe that most lawyers overcharge. While the generalization about lawyers may or may not be true, relying on such experiences as the basis for a general belief is a mistake! Because a single personal experience, or even an accumulation of personal experiences, is not enough to give you a *representative* sample of experiences, personal experiences often lead us to commit the Hasty Generalization fallacy. A single striking experience or several such experiences can demonstrate that certain outcomes are *possible;* for example, you may have met several people who smoked three packs of cigarettes a day and lived to the age of 90. Such experiences, however, can't demonstrate that such outcomes are *typical* or *probable.*

---

F: **Hasty Generalization Fallacy:** A person draws a conclusion about a large group based on experiences with only a few members of the group.

---

We will revisit this fallacy in Chapter 9 when we discuss research evidence and issues of sampling.

## Personal Testimonials as Evidence

"You should see Dr. Feelgood for your surgery. He did a great job on my shoulder."

"I had cancer and was told by my doctor that I had just one month to live; but after just one visit with my spiritual healer, my cancer disappeared. You should consider stopping your radiation treatment and visit this woman."

"In only six weeks, I lost ten pounds, using Lesflab. I highly recommend it to you."

"Look at me; I'm tired all the time, all my joints hurt, I have a skin rash, and can't remember anything since returning from the war. Don't tell me there's no such thing as a Gulf War Syndrome."

Commercials, ads for movies, recommendations on the backs of book jackets, and "proofs" of the existence of the paranormal or other controversial or extraordinary life events often try to persuade by using a particular kind of appeal to personal experience; they quote particular persons as saying that a given idea or product is good or bad, or that extraordinary events have occurred, based upon their personal experiences. Such quoted statements serve as *personal testimonials.*

How helpful is such evidence? Usually, it is not very helpful at all. In most cases we should pay little attention to personal testimonials until we find out much more about the expertise, interests, values, and biases behind them. We should be especially wary of each of the following problems with testimonials:

* **Selectivity.** People's experiences differ greatly. Those trying to persuade us have usually carefully selected the testimony they use. We should always ask the question, "What was the experience like for those whom we have not heard from?" Also, the people who provide the testimonials have often been selective in their attention, paying special attention to information that confirms their beliefs and ignoring disconfirming information. Often, believing is seeing! Our *expectancies* greatly influence how we experience events. If we believe that Bigfoot is out there someplace, or that angels leave signs for us, then we are more likely to see ambiguous images as Bigfoot or as angel signs.

* **Personal interest.** Many testimonials, such as those used for books, movies, and television products come from people who have something to gain from their testimony. For example, authors will sometimes provide positive testimonials for others, expecting a return of the favor when their book is reviewed. Thus, we need to ask, "Does the person providing the testimony have a relationship with what she is advocating such that we can expect a strong bias in her testimony?"

- **Omitted information.** Testimonials rarely provide sufficient information about the basis for the judgment. For example, when a friend of yours raves about a teacher, you would want to ask why he was so impressed. Our standards may differ from the standards of those giving the testimony. We often have too little information to decide whether we should treat such claims seriously.

- **The human factor.** One reason that testimonials are so convincing is that they come from human beings and they are very vivid and detailed, a marked contrast to statistics and graphs, which tend to be very abstract. They are often provided by very enthusiastic people, who seem trustworthy, well-meaning, and honest. Such people make us *want* to believe them.

## Appeals to Authority as Evidence

A speaker makes the claim that Ford cars are superior to General Motors cars. When we ask him how he knows, he says, "*Consumer Reports* says so, and also an article I saw in *The New York Times* last week claimed that Ford makes better cars."

The speaker has defended his claim by appealing to authority—sources that are supposed to know more than most of us about a given topic—so-called experts. When communicators appeal to authorities or experts, they appeal to people who they believe are in a position to have access to certain facts and to have special qualifications for drawing conclusions from the facts. You encounter appeals to many forms of authority on a daily basis.

> Movie reviewers: "One of the ten best movies of the year." Valerie Viewer, *Toledo Gazette.*
>
> Organizations: "The American Medical Association supports this position."
>
> Researchers: "Studies show . . ."
>
> Relatives: "My grandfather says . . ."
>
> Religion: "The Koran says . . ."
>
> Magazines: "According to *Newsweek* . . ."
>
> College professors: "The appropriate interpretation of Plato is . . ."
>
> Expert witnesses: "It is my belief that the defendant . . ."

You can easily add to our list. It should be obvious that some appeals to authority should be taken much more seriously as evidence than others. Why?

Some authorities are much more careful in giving an opinion than others. For example, *Newsweek* and *Time* are much more likely to carefully evaluate the available evidence prior to stating an opinion than is *The National Enquirer*. Articles on depression are more likely to be based on carefully collected evidence if they posted on the National Institute of Mental Health Web site than if they are posted on a personal Web page. Our relatives are much less likely than editorial writers for major newspapers to have systematically evaluated a political candidate.

You should remember that for many reasons, *authorities are often wrong*. Also, they often disagree. The following examples, taken from *The Experts Speak*, are clear reminders of the fallibility of expert opinion (Christopher Cerf and Victor Navasky, 1998, Rev. Ed., Villard Books, New York).

"It is once and for all clear . . . that the earth is in the middle of the world and all weights move towards it." Ptolemy (Alexandrian astronomer and geographer), *The Almagest*, second century A.D., page 5.

"Nature intended women to be our slaves . . . They are our property . . . They belong to us, just as a tree that bears fruit belongs to a gardener. What a mad idea to demand equality for women! . . . Women are nothing but machines for producing children." Napoleon Bonaparte (1769–1821), page 32.

"Video won't be able to hold onto any market it captures after the first six months. People will soon get tired of staring at a plywood box every night." Darryl F. Zanuck (Head of Twentieth Century Fox Studios), ca. 1946, page 41.

"If excessive smoking actually plays a role in the production of lung cancer, it seems to be a minor one." Dr. W. C. Heuper (National Cancer Institute), quoted in *The New York Times*, April 14, 1954, page 228.

These quotes should remind us that we need to ask critical questions when communicators appeal to authority. We need to ask, *"Why should we believe this authority?"* More specifically, we should ask the following questions of authorities.

*How much expertise or training does the authority have on the subject about which he is communicating?* For example, is this a topic the person has studied for a long time? Or, has the person had extensive experience related to the topic?

*Was the authority in a position to have especially good access to pertinent facts?* For example, was she a firsthand observer of the events about which she makes claims? Or, has a newspaper reporter, for example, actually witnessed an event, or has she merely relied upon reports from others? If the authority is not a firsthand observer, whose claims is she repeating? Why should we rely on those claims? In general, you should be more impressed by *primary sources*—or direct observers—than by *secondary sources,* those who are relying on others for their evidence. *Time* and *Newsweek,* for example, are secondary sources, while research journals such as the *Journal of the American Medical Association* are primary sources.

*Is there good reason to believe that the authority is relatively free of distorting influences?* Among the factors that can influence how evidence is reported are personal needs, prior expectations, general beliefs, attitudes, values, theories, and ideologies. These can subconsciously or deliberately affect how evidence is presented. For example, if a general in the military is asked whether cuts in military spending are bad for the military, he may answer "yes" and give a number of good reasons. He may be giving an unbiased view of the situation. Because of his position, however, we would want to be concerned about the possibility that he has sought out reasons to justify his own biases.

By bias and prejudice, we mean possessing a strong personal feeling about the goodness or badness of something, such that it interferes with our ability to evaluate it fairly. Because many factors bias us in virtually all our judgments, we cannot expect any authority to be *totally* unbiased. We can, however, expect less bias from some authorities than from others and try to determine such bias by seeking information about the authority's personal interest in the topic under discussion. For example, we want to be especially wary when an authority stands to benefit financially from the actions she advocates.

Because an authority can have a personal interest in an issue and still make dependable claims, we should not reject a claim simply because we suspect that the authority's personal interests may interfere with her fairness. One helpful step we can take is to check to see whether authorities with diverse attitudes, prior expectations, values, and interests agree. Thus we need to ask the questions: *"Has the authority developed a reputation for frequently making dependable claims? Have we been able to rely on this authority in the past?"*

You will want to be especially concerned about the quality of authorities when you encounter factual claims on the Internet. There, virtually everyone becomes an "authority," because people are free to claim whatever they wish, and there is no built-in process to evaluate such claims. It is clearly a "buyer beware" situation!

## USING THIS CRITICAL QUESTION

When you identify problems with intuition, personal experience, testimonials, and appeals to authority as evidence, you then have a proper basis for hesitating to accept the conclusion based on that evidence. Knowing these problems gives you some protection against bogus reasoning. However, you do want to work hard to be fair to the arguments that people present for your consideration. So it makes sense to ask those who provide you with insubstantial evidence whether they can give you some better evidence. Give arguments every chance they deserve.

## Summary

---

### Clues for Evaluating the Evidence

Use the following questions to help assess the various kinds of evidence.

**Intuition**

? Does the intuition have any other kind of evidential support?

**Authority**

? How much expertise or training does the authority have on this particular subject?

? Was the authority in a position to have especially good access to pertinent facts?

? Is there good reason to believe that the authority is relatively free of distorting influences?

? Has the authority developed a reputation for frequently making dependable claims?

? Have we been able to rely on this authority in the past?

**Personal Testimony**

? What biases or interests might be affecting the person's testimony?

? Does the person have any expertise to assist his or her judgment?

? How do the person's value assumptions affect his or her testimony?

? Whose personal testimony might be helpful in assessing this person's testimony?

? What information has been left out in this personal testimony?

---

In this chapter, we have focused on the evaluation of several kinds of evidence used to support factual claims: intuition, personal experience, personal testimonials, and appeals to authorities. Such evidence must be relied on with caution. We have provided you with some questions you should ask to determine whether such evidence is *good evidence.* In the next chapter, we discuss other kinds of evidence, as we continue to ask the question, *"How good is the evidence?"*

## Practice Exercises

 *Critical Question:* **How good is the evidence: intuition, personal experience, testimonials, and appeals to authority?**

Evaluate the evidence in the following three passages.

### Passage 1

While educational costs skyrocket, students are getting less and less for their money. They are paying $20,000 a year for their education; but they are not getting the teaching they think they are paying for. Professors are putting their time and energy into research, not into teaching. Consider the following comments from students attending a major research university.

Sandra W., sophomore English major: "You sit in classes with three hundred other students while you listen to a graduate student who can't even speak English."

Lori L., junior psychology major and honors student: "I've been in college over three years, and I still haven't had any one-to-one contact with a professor."

John M., freshman philosophy major: "It's impossible to find professors when you need them. One professor of mine was on campus only one day a week."

### Passage 2

Are silicone breast implants dangerous? It looks as if women who have had such surgery can again feel safe. In a recent interview, Dr. Walter Newbody, a nationally known West Coast plastic surgeon, stated that implants are perfectly safe. He reports that in 10 years of performing silicone-gel implants, he has noted no serious problems resulting from the implants. Furthermore, the Southwestern Association of Plastic Surgery has declared in a recent publication that implants do not trigger autoimmune disorders, despite the claims of some physicians.

### Passage 3

At some point in most young peoples' lives the idea of being a lawyer comes to mind. And of those people, most of them go to college with this idea in mind. For some reason this country is shoulder-deep in future lawyers, many of whom cannot find work. Dr. Sharpe, professor of law, says, "My law classes are absolutely full of students. Every desk is full."

*Time* magazine reports there are three times as many law students as there are lawyers in the country. In addition, nearly 60 percent of law students will not find jobs within their major.

Why is there such an attraction for this profession? It is mostly money. A Harvard survey of a randomly sampled group of first-year law students says that nearly 70 percent of people polled said that the high salary was the main attraction. The truth of the matter, however, is that most lawyers do not make much money at all. Myron Nickle, a lawyer for 15 years, says, "I have never made more than $45,000 a year. This notion of being a high-powered lawyer in New York is totally glamorized in TV and the movies."

## Sample Responses

### Passage 1

CONCLUSION: *Students at major research universities are not getting their money's worth.*

REASON: *Three students voice their dissatisfaction with the teaching they are receiving.*

Although the general conclusion may or may not be accurate, we should not rely on these testimonials as good "proof." This passage illustrates well the weaknesses of testimony as evidence. How typical are these "horror stories"? Would other students have raved about their teachers? How were the interviews conducted? Is the author's selection of interview comments biased? Did the students know what the interviewer was trying to prove and thus try to please the interviewer? Before we conclude that students were being cheated in their education, we would want much better evidence than just a few testimonials. What the testimonials do tell us, however, is that it is possible for students to have bad experiences with teachers at this university.

### Passage 2

CONCLUSION: *Breast implants are safe.*

REASON: *A surgeon and a state professional organization claim implants are safe.*

How much should we depend on these appeals to authority? Not much. First, both authorities are likely to be very biased. They stand to gain financially by making safety claims. Dr. Newbody's testimony is especially suspect because it is based on his experiences only. He has probably not sought out evidence of failures. We might pay more attention to the claims of the state professional organization if it were to provide us with the research information on which its claim is based.

# 9

# How Good Is the Evidence: Personal Observation, Research Studies, Case Examples, and Analogies?

In this chapter, we continue our evaluation of evidence. We focus on four common kinds of evidence: personal observation, research studies, case examples, and analogies. We need to question each of these as we encounter them as evidence.

[?] *Critical Question:* **How good is the evidence: personal observation, research studies, case examples, and analogies?**

## Personal Observation

One valuable kind of evidence is personal observation, the basis for much scientific research. For example, we feel confident of something we actually see. Thus, we highly value eyewitness testimony as evidence. A difficulty with personal observation, however, is the tendency to see or hear what we wish to see or hear, selecting and remembering those aspects of an experience that are most consistent with our previous experience and background.

Observers, unlike certain mirrors, do not give us "pure" observations. What we "see" and report is filtered through a set of values, biases, attitudes, and expectations. Because of such influences, observers often disagree about what they perceive. Thus, we should be wary of reliance on observations made by any single observer in situations in which we might expect observations among observers to vary.

Three illustrations should help you see the danger of relying on personal observation as evidence:

- An umpire sees a strike; the batter sees a ball.

- A robbery occurs in a convenience store. One witness claims to have seen a large pistol in the hands of the perpetrator; another witness swears that the robber was waving a squirt gun in the air.

- One friend sees the comments you made to your significant other as hostile; another friend remarks that you are admirably assertive.

While personal observations can often be valuable sources of evidence, we need to recognize that they are not unbiased "mirrors of reality"; and when they are used to support controversial conclusions, we should seek verification by other observers as well as other kinds of evidence to support the conclusion. For example, if someone claims that she saw a teacher act in a sexually suggestive way toward a student, the evidence becomes much stronger if other students verify the observation. Also, remember that observational reports get increasingly problematic as the time between the observation and the report of the observation increases.

When reports of observations in newspapers, magazines, books, television, and the Internet are used as evidence, you need to determine whether there are good reasons to rely on such reports. The most reliable reports will be based on recent observations, made by someone observing under optimal conditions and someone who is not likely to have strong expectations or biases related to the event being observed.

## Research Studies as Evidence

"Studies show . . ."

"Research investigators have found in a recent survey that . . ."

"A report in the *New England Journal of Medicine* indicates . . ."

One form of authority that relies a great deal on observation and often carries special weight is the research study: usually a systematic collection of observations by people trained to do scientific research. How dependable are research findings? Like appeals to any authority, we can't tell about the dependability of research findings until we ask lots of questions.

Society has turned to the scientific method as an important guide for determining the facts because the relationships among events in our world are very complex, and because humans are fallible in their observations and theories about these events. The scientific method attempts to avoid many of the built-in biases in our observations of the world and in our intuition and common sense.

What is special about the scientific method? Above all, it seeks information in the form of *publicly verifiable data*—that is, data obtained under conditions such that other qualified people can make similar observations and see whether they get the same results. Thus, for example, if one researcher reports that a new radiation treatment kills cancer cells, we can have much more confidence in that treatment if other researchers repeat the experiment and get the same results.

A second major characteristic of scientific method is *control*—that is, the using of special procedures to reduce error in observations and in the interpretation of research findings. For example, if bias in observations may be a major problem, researchers might try to control this kind of error by using multiple observers to see how well they agree with one another. Physical scientists frequently maximize control by studying problems in the laboratory so that they can minimize extraneous factors. Unfortunately, control is usually more difficult in the social world than in the physical world; thus it is very difficult to successfully apply the scientific method to many questions about complex human behavior.

*Precision in language* is a third major component of the scientific method. Our concepts are often confusing, obscure, and ambiguous. Scientific method tries to be precise and consistent in its use of language.

While there is much more to science than we can discuss here, we want you to keep in mind that scientific research, when conducted well, is one of our best sources of evidence because it emphasizes verifiability, control, and precision.

## Problems with Research Findings

Unfortunately, the fact that research has been applied to a problem does not necessarily mean that the research evidence is dependable evidence or that the interpretations of the meaning of the evidence are accurate. Like appeals to any source, appeals to research evidence must be approached with caution. Also, some questions, particularly those that focus on human behavior, can be answered only tentatively even with the best of evidence. Thus, there are a number of important questions we want to ask about research studies before we decide how much we want to depend on their conclusions.

When communicators appeal to research as a source of evidence, you should remember the following:

1. Research varies greatly in *quality;* we should rely more on some research studies than others. There is well-done research and there is poorly done research, and we should rely more on the former. Because the research process is so complex and subject to so many external influences, even those well-trained in research practices sometimes conduct research studies that have important deficiencies; publication in a scientific journal does not guarantee that a research study is not flawed in important ways.

2. Research findings often contradict one another. Thus, *single* research studies presented out of the context of the family of research studies that investigate the question often provide misleading conclusions. Research findings that most deserve our attention are those that have been repeated by more than one researcher or group of researchers. We need to always ask the question: "Have other researchers verified the findings?"

3. Research findings *do not prove* conclusions. At best, they *support* conclusions. Research findings do not speak for themselves! Researchers must always *interpret* the meaning of their findings, and all findings can be interpreted in more than one way. Thus, researchers' conclusions should not be treated as demonstrated "truths." When you encounter statements such as "research findings show . . ." you should retranslate them into "researchers interpret their research findings as showing . . ."

4. Like all of us, researchers have expectations, attitudes, values, and needs that bias the questions they ask, the way they conduct their research, and the way they interpret their research findings. Despite its best efforts to avoid bias, science is not a neutral, value-free, totally objective enterprise. For example, scientists often have an emotional investment in a particular hypothesis. Like all fallible human beings, they may find it difficult to objectively treat data that conflict with that hypothesis. A major strength of scientific research is that it tries to make public its procedures and results so that others can judge the merit of the research and then try to replicate it. However, regardless of how objective a scientific report may seem, important subjective elements are always involved.

5.  Speakers and writers often distort or simplify research conclusions. Major discrepancies may occur between the conclusion merited by the original research and the use of the evidence to support a communicator's beliefs. For example, researchers may carefully qualify their own conclusions in their original research report only to have the conclusions used by others without the qualifications.

6.  Research "facts" change over time, especially claims about human behavior. For example, all of the following research "facts" have been reported by major scientific sources, yet have been "refuted" by recent research evidence:

Left-handed people die at a younger age than right-handed people.

Women under age 50 benefit from mammograms.

A gene has been found that causes manic-depressive disorder.

Fiber helps prevent colon cancer.

The damaging effects of divorce on children are cumulative.

7.  Research varies in how artificial it is. Often, to achieve the goal of control, research loses some of its "real-world" quality. The more artificial the research, the more difficult it is to generalize from the research study to the world outside. The problem of research artificiality is especially evident in research studying complex social behavior. For example, to study the effects of television violence, researchers may expose children to violent cartoons and afterward observe how aggressive they are toward dolls. We should ask, "Is aggressive behavior toward dolls too artificial to tell us much about aggressive behavior in other situations?"

8.  The need for financial gain, status, security, and other factors can affect research outcomes. Researchers are human beings, not computers. Thus, it is extremely difficult for them to be totally objective. For example, researchers getting directly funded by major drug companies may more frequently find positive treatment results for that company's drugs than researchers who have no personal relationship with the drug company. Also, pressures to get tenure and promotions, to maintain large grants, and to become famous may all influence the objectivity of the research findings.

As you can see, despite the many positive qualities of research evidence, we need to avoid embracing research conclusions prematurely.

## Clues for Evaluating Research Studies

Apply these questions to research findings to determine whether the findings are dependable evidence.

1.  *What is the quality of the source of the report?* Usually, the most dependable reports are those published in peer-review journals, those in which a study is not accepted until it has been reviewed by a series of relevant experts. Usually—but not always—the more reputable the source, the better designed the study. So, try to find out all you can about the reputation of the source.

2.  Other than the quality of the source, are there other clues included in the communication suggesting the research was well done? For example, *does the report detail any special strengths of the research?*

3.  *Has the study been replicated?* Has more than one study reached the same conclusion? Findings, even when "statistically significant," can arise by chance alone. For example, when an association is repeatedly and consistently found in well-designed studies, like the link between smoking and cancer, then there is reason to believe it, at least until those who disagree can provide persuasive evidence for their point of view.

4.  *How selective has the communicator been in choosing studies?* For example, have relevant studies with contradictory results been omitted? Has the researcher selected only those studies that support her point?

5.  *Is there any evidence of strong-sense critical thinking?* Has the speaker or writer showed a critical attitude toward earlier research that was supportive of her point of view? Most conclusions from research need to be qualified because of research limitations. Has the communicator demonstrated a willingness to qualify?

6.  *Is there any reason for someone to have distorted the research?* We need to be wary of situations in which the researchers *need* to find certain kinds of results.

7.  *Are conditions in the research artificial and therefore distorted?* Always ask, "How similar are the conditions under which the research study was conducted to the situation the researcher is generalizing about?"

8.  *How far can we generalize, given the research sample?* We discuss this question in depth in our next section.

9.  *Are there any biases or distortions in the surveys, questionnaires, ratings, or other measurements that the researcher uses?* We need to have confidence that the researcher has measured accurately what she has wanted to measure. The problem of biased surveys and questionnaires is so pervasive in research that we discuss it in more detail in a later section.

## Generalizing from the Research Sample

Speakers and writers usually use research reports to support generalizations, that is, claims about events in general. For example, "Divorce was harmful to the children in the Jones family" is NOT a generalization, but "Divorce is harmful to children" is. The ability to generalize from research findings depends on the *number, breadth,* and *randomness* of events or people the researchers study.

The process of selecting events or persons to study is called *sampling.*

Because researchers can never study all events or people about which they want to generalize, they must choose some way to sample; and some ways are preferable to others. You need to keep several important considerations in mind when evaluating the research sample:

1.  The sample must be large enough to justify the generalization or conclusion. In most cases, the more events or people researchers observe, the more dependable their conclusion. If we want to form a general belief about how often college students receive help from others on term papers, we are better off studying 100 college students than studying 10.

2.  The sample must possess as much *breadth,* or diversity, as the types of events about which conclusions are to be drawn. For example, if researchers want to generalize about college students' drinking habits in general, their evidence should be based on the sampling of a variety of different kinds of college students in a variety of different kinds of college settings. Students at a small private school in the Midwest may have different drinking habits than students at a large public school on the West Coast; thus, a study of students attending only one school would lack breadth of sampling.

3.  The more *random* the sample, the better. When researchers randomly sample, they try to make sure that all events about which they want to generalize have an *equal chance* of getting sampled; they try to avoid a

biased sample. Major polls, like the Gallop poll, for example, always try to sample randomly. This keeps them from getting groups of events or people that have biased characteristics. Do you see how each of the following samples has biased characteristics?

a. People who volunteer to be interviewed about frequency of sexual activity.

b. People who are at home at 2:30 P.M. to answer their phone.

c. Readers of a popular women's magazine who clip and complete mail-in surveys.

Thus, we want to ask of all research studies, *"How many events or people did they sample, how much breadth did the sample have, and how random was the sample?"*

A common problem that stems from not paying enough attention to the limits of sampling is for communicators to *overgeneralize* research findings. They state a generalization that is much broader than that warranted by the research. In Chapter 7, we referred to such overgeneralizing as the *Hasty Generalization* fallacy. Let's take a close look at a research overgeneralization:

> Verbal abuse by professors is rampant on our campuses. A recent survey of 300 females at Brightsville College found that over 20 percent of them reported they had been verbally abused by at least one professor.

Sampling procedures prohibit such a broad generalization. The research report implies the conclusion can be applied to *all* campuses, when the research studied only one campus. We don't even know whether the conclusion can be applied to that campus, because we don't know how randomly researchers sampled from it. The research report is flawed because it greatly overgeneralizes.

Remember: *We can generalize only to people and events that are like those that we have studied in the research!*

Be alert to the possibility of overgeneralizing! It is a pervasive and powerful human disposition against which we must continually struggle.

## Biased Surveys and Questionnaires

It's early evening. You have just finished dinner. The phone rings. "We're conducting a survey of public opinion. Will you answer a few questions?" If you answer "yes," you will be among thousands who annually take part in surveys— one of the research methods you will encounter most frequently. Think how often you hear the phrase "according to recent polls."

Surveys and questionnaires are usually used to measure people's attitudes and beliefs. Just how dependable are they? It depends! Survey responses are subject to many influences; thus, one has to be very cautious in interpreting their meaning. Let's examine some of these influences.

First, for survey responses to be meaningful, they must be answered honestly. That is, verbal reports need to mirror actual beliefs and attitudes. Yet, for a variety of reasons, people frequently shade the truth. For example, they may give answers they think they ought to give, rather than answers that reflect their true beliefs. They may experience hostility toward the questionnaire or toward the kind of question asked. They may give too little thought to the question. If you have ever been a survey participant, you can probably think of other influences.

Remember: *You cannot assume that verbal reports accurately reflect true attitudes.*

Second, many survey questions are ambiguous in their wording; the questions are subject to multiple interpretations. Different individuals may in essence be responding to different questions! For example, imagine the multiple possible interpretations of the following survey question: "Are you happily married?" The more ambiguous the wording of a survey, the less credibility you can place in the results.

You should always ask the question: "How were the survey questions worded?" Usually, the more specifically worded a question, the more likely that different individuals will interpret it similarly.

Third, surveys contain many *built-in biases* that make them even more suspect. Two of the most important are *biased wording* and *biased context.* Biased wording of a question is a common problem; a small change in how a question is asked can have a major effect on how a question is answered. Let's examine a conclusion based on a recent poll and then look at the survey question.

A U.S. congressman sent a questionnaire to his constituents and received the following results: 92 percent were against government-supported child-care centers.

Now let's look closely at the survey question: "Do you believe the federal government should provide child-care centers to assist parents in rearing their children?" Look carefully at this question. Do you see the built-in bias? The "leading" words are "to assist parents in rearing their children." Wouldn't the responses have been quite different if the question had read: "Do you believe the federal government should provide child-care centers to assist parents who are unable to find alternative child care while they are working?" Thus, the responses obtained here are not an accurate indicator of attitudes concerning child-care centers.

Survey data and questionnaire must always be examined for possible bias. *Look carefully at the wording of the questions!* Here is another example. We have emphasized the word that evidences the bias.

> QUESTION: *Do you think that a person with a homosexual* disorder *should be permitted to teach your innocent children?*

> CONCLUSION: *Seventy-five percent of the people do not want homosexuals to teach their children.*

The effect of *context* on an answer to a question can also be powerful. Even answers to identical questions can vary from poll to poll depending on how the questionnaire is presented and how the question is embedded in the survey. The following question was included in two recent surveys: "Do you think it should be possible for a pregnant woman to obtain a legal abortion if she is married and does not want any more children?" In one survey, the question was preceded by another question: "Should a woman be allowed to have an abortion if she had evidence that the fetus was defective?" In the other survey, no preceding question occurred. Not surprisingly, the two surveys showed different results. Can you see how the context might have affected respondents?

Another important contextual factor is *length*. In long surveys, people may respond differently to later items than to earlier items simply because they get tired. *Be alert to contextual factors when evaluating survey results.*

Because the way people respond to surveys is affected by many unknown factors, such as the need to please or the interpretation of the question, should we ever treat survey evidence as good evidence? There are heated debates about this issue, but our answer is "yes," as long as we are careful and do not generalize further than warranted. Some surveys are more reputable than others. The better the quality of the survey, the more you should be influenced by the results. Our recommendation is to examine survey *procedures* carefully before accepting survey *results*. Once you have ascertained the quality of the procedures, you can choose to generate your own *qualified generalization*—one that takes into account any biases you might have found. For example, if a survey has been completed using subscribers to a magazine associated with a liberal ideology then you would want to restrict any generalization found to people subscribing to that magazine. Even biased surveys can be informative; but you need to know the biases in order not to be unduly persuaded by the findings.

# Critical Evaluation of a Research-Based Argument

Let's now use our questions about research to evaluate the following argument in which research evidence has been used to support a conclusion.

> Parents who try to keep their children from getting fat may wind up producing kids who don't know how to stop eating when they've had enough, a new study suggests. The study of 77 children ages 3 to 5 found that those with the most body fat had the most "controlling" mothers when it came to the amount of food eaten. "The more control the mother reported using over her child's eating, the less self-regulation the child displayed," Johnson and co-author Leann L. Birch said in the November issue of *Pediatrics*. The study was done at a preschool at the University of Illinois at Champaign-Urbana. The study found children whose mothers allowed them to be most spontaneous about food, eat when they are hungry, and not necessarily finish all the food given to them showed a natural instinct for regulating their own calories, the researchers said. "These internal cues, when interrupted, may well lead to overeating in later childhood, which could contribute to the child being overweight" said a pediatric nutritionist at Stanford University Medical Center.

In this communication, the research is presented in an uncritical fashion. We see no sign of strong-sense critical thinking. The communication uncritically accepts the findings. The original research study was published in a reputable journal, suggesting that it should be of high quality. The report makes no references to special strengths or weaknesses of the study, although it does provides some detail about the research procedures so that we can make judgments about its worth as the basis of a generalization. There is no indication of whether the study has been replicated. Also, we do not know how selective the communicator has been in choosing studies, nor how this research fits into the broader context of research on causes of obesity. We do not know what benefits publishing this study may have had for the researchers, but we might speculate that publishing such research may help facilitate their getting grants or promotions, perhaps making them less cautious in making interpretations of their findings.

Have the researchers and passage author overgeneralized? The sample is small—77—and it lacks breadth and randomness because it is restricted to one preschool in the Midwest. We need to ask many questions about the sampling. How were these children selected? How was the study advertised to the parents? Could there have been a bias in the kind of parents willing to sign up for such a study? Would we have gotten similar results if we had randomly chosen families from a large number of schools throughout the country? This passage clearly illustrates a case of overgeneralization!

Are the questionnaires biased? Contemplate being a parent and completing a questionnaire about how controlling you are. Don't you think we could raise doubts about the accuracy of responses to such a questionnaire? Too little information is given about the wording of the questionnaires or about the arrangement of questionnaire items to judge the ambiguity of the item wording and the possibility of biased wording and biased context.

We have raised enough questions about the above passage to be wary of its factual claims. We would want to rely on much more research before we could conclude that these claims are dependable.

Let's now look at a very different source of evidence.

## Case Examples as Evidence

Presidential candidate speaking: "Our party's program has done wonders for women in our country. In fact in our audience is Alice Goodcase, a 70-year-old woman who has flown all the way from a small town in Southern Illinois to be with us today. Alice is now working a full time job at a hospital because of our new job stimulus program for the elderly. Alice, would you please stand?"

A frequently used kind of evidence that contrasts markedly to the kind of research study that we have just described, which emphasized studying large representative samples, is the use of a detailed description of one or several particular individuals or events to support a conclusion. Such descriptions are usually based on observations or interviews and vary from being in depth and thorough to being superficial. We call such descriptions *case examples.*

Communicators often begin persuasive presentations with dramatic descriptions of cases. For example, one way to argue that stricter gun control laws are needed is to provide vivid case study descriptions of innocent people who have been killed by guns.

Case examples are often compelling to us because of their colorfulness, and their interesting details, which make them easy to visualize. Political candidates have increasingly resorted to case examples in their speeches, knowing that the rich details of cases generate an emotional reaction. Such cases, however, should be viewed more as *striking examples or anecdotes* than as proof, and we must be very suspicious of their use as evidence.

Dramatic cases *appeal to our emotions* and distract us from seeking other more relevant research evidence. For example, a detailed description of an obese welfare mother who has been irresponsible, has lived on welfare for 10 years, has lived with multiple husbands, and has had children by each of them may lead us to ignore the more relevant statistical data that only 10 percent of welfare recipients remain on welfare rolls for four years or longer.

*Be wary of striking case examples as proof!*

Although case examples will be consistent with a conclusion, do not let that consistency fool you. Always ask yourself: "Is the example typical?" "Are there powerful counterexamples?" "Are there biases in how the example is exported?"

Are there times that case examples can be useful, even if they are not good evidence? Certainly! Like personal experiences, they demonstrate important *possibilities,* and put a personal face on abstract statistics. They make it easier for people to relate to an issue and thus take more interest in it.

## Analogies as Evidence

Look closely at the structure of the following brief arguments, paying special attention to the reason supporting the conclusion.

> Education cannot prepare men and women for marriage. Trying to educate them for marriage is like trying to teach them to swim without allowing them to go into the water. It cannot be done.

> Who is responsible for all this unethical behavior in the present administration? It must be the president. After all, a fish rots from the head down.

> You wouldn't want to ingest a spoonful of arsenic into your system daily. I do not understand why you keep smoking. They both can kill you.

These three arguments use *analogies* as evidence, a very different kind of evidence from what we have previously been evaluating. How do we decide whether it is good evidence? Before reading on, try to determine the persuasiveness of the three arguments.

Communicators often attempt to prove a conclusion about something with which they are relatively *unfamiliar* by relying upon its similarity to something with which they are familiar. They use *resemblance* as a form of evidence. They reason in the following way: "If these two things are alike in one respect, then they will probably be alike in other respects as well."

For example, when researchers were first seeking the cause of AIDS, they identified diseases that seemed to share some similarities with AIDS, such as hepatitis, and tried to infer conclusions about the cause of AIDS on the basis of what they knew about the causes of these other diseases. We reason in a similar fashion when we choose to see a movie because a friend recommends it. We reason that because we resemble each other in a number of likes and dislikes, we will enjoy the same movie.

We will refer to an argument that uses a well-known similarity between two things as the basis for a conclusion about a relatively unknown characteristic of one of those things as an *argument by analogy*. Reasoning by analogy is a common way of presenting evidence to support a conclusion.

Analogies both stimulate insights and deceive us. For example, analogies have been highly productive in scientific and legal reasoning. When we infer conclusions about humans on the basis of research with mice, we reason by analogy. Much of our thinking about the structure of the atom is analogical reasoning. When we make a decision in a legal case, we may base that decision on the similarity of that case to preceding cases. For example, when judges approach the question of whether a ban on flag-burning violates the constitutional protection against laws abridging freedom of speech, they must decide whether flag-burning is analogous to freedom of speech; thus, they reason by analogy. Such reasoning can be quite insightful and persuasive.

Analogical reasoning can also be quite deceptive. A former leader of a European country, for example, used an analogy to defend executing people convicted of adultery, prostitution, and homosexuality:

> If your finger suffers from gangrene, what do you do? You don't let the whole hand and then the body become filled with gangrene. No, you chop the finger off. So it is with corruption. We have to eliminate corruption.

Are gangrene and adultery, prostitution, and homosexuality *that* similar? Not at all. Thus, we have a very deceptive analogy. When certain societies burned people as though they were "witches," they acted on faulty analogical reasoning.

### Evaluating Analogies

Because analogical reasoning is so common and has the potential to be both persuasive and faulty, you will find it very useful to recognize such reasoning and know how to systematically evaluate it. To evaluate the quality of an analogy, you need to focus on two factors.

1. The number of ways the two things being compared are similar and different.
2. The *relevance* of the similarities and the differences.

A word of caution: You can almost always find some similarities between any two things. So, analogical reasoning will not be persuasive simply because of many similarities. Strong analogies will be ones in which the two things we compare possess relevant similarities and lack relevant differences. All analogies try to illustrate underlying principles. *Relevant similarities and differences are ones that directly relate to the underlying principle illustrated by the analogy.*

Let's check out the soundness of the following argument by analogy.

> I do not send my son outside when he is sick with flu or measles. Why should parents want to send their youngsters with AIDS to school? Do these children feel like running, jumping, and playing when they are ill? You do not let your child go to school with the measles, so keep him at home if he has AIDS. After all, he is sick.

A major similarity between measles and AIDS that is potentially relevant to sending children to school is "having an illness." We note some relevant differences, however. Measles is associated with severe symptoms that gradually disappear, and the measles virus is easily transferred from one person to another. Development of symptoms from AIDS is very unpredictable, and there may be long periods without acute symptoms. It is not highly communicable because it is transferred through the blood. Thus, children with AIDS often feel well enough to want to attend school and, given our present state of knowledge, seem highly unlikely to pass the disease on to others. Because these differences should have some impact upon whether we keep a child out of school, they are relevant; thus, the analogy fails to provide strong support for the conclusion.

Another strategy that may help you evaluate reasoning by analogy is to *generate alternative analogies* for understanding the same phenomenon that the author or speaker is trying to understand. Such analogies may either support or contradict the conclusions inferred from the original analogy. If they contradict the conclusion, they then reveal problems in the initial reasoning by analogy.

For example, when authors argue that alcoholics should be eligible for health insurance, sick leave, and other benefits associated with inadvertent disease, they use a particular analogy to infer conclusions about alcoholics: alcoholism is like a biologically caused disease. Others, however, have generated an alternative analogy, arguing that alcoholism is like a "breakdown of the will." Note how thinking about this different analogy may create doubts about the persuasiveness of the original analogy.

A productive way to generate your own analogies is the following:

1.  Identify some important features of what you are studying.

2.  Try to identify other situations with which you are familiar that have some similar features. Give free rein to your imagination. Brainstorm. Try to imagine diverse situations.

**3.** Try to determine whether the familiar situation can provide you with some insights about the unfamiliar situation.

For example, in thinking about alcoholism, you could try to think of other situations in which people repeatedly seek immediate gratification despite potential long-term negative effects. Do smoking, eating, or gambling come to mind? Do they trigger other ways to think about alcoholism? You should now be capable of systematically evaluating the three brief analogical arguments at the beginning of this section. Ask the questions you need to ask to determine the structure of the argument. Then, ask the questions to evaluate the argument. Look for relevant similarities and differences. Usually, the greater the ratio of relevant similarities to relevant differences, the stronger the analogy. An analogy is especially compelling if you can find *no* relevant difference and you can find good evidence that the relevant similarities do indeed exist.

We found a relevant difference that weakens each of our three initial sample analogies. Check your evaluation against our list.

(First example) The primary skills required for successful swimming are motor skills; many skills required for a successful marriage differ from motor skills. Such skills as money management and communication can be learned outside the context of marriage.

(Second example) The "parts" of a political administration function much more independently than the parts of a fish. Unethical behavior at lower levels can result from complex and diverse causes.

(Third example) In the case of arsenic, death is immediate and certain; in the case of smoking, death is statistically neither immediate nor certain. Also, smoking provides a great deal of immediate satisfaction; arsenic does not.

Analogies that trick or deceive us fit our definition of a reasoning fallacy; such deception is called the Faulty Analogy fallacy.

---

F: **Faulty Analogy:**     Occurs when an analogy is proposed in which there are important relevant dissimilarities.

---

In one sense, all analogies are faulty, because they make the mistaken assumption that because two things are alike in one or more respects, they are necessarily alike in some other important respect. It is probably best for you to think of analogies as varying from very weak to very strong. But even the best analogies are only suggestive. Thus if an author draws a conclusion about one case from a comparison to another case, then she should provide further evidence to support the principle revealed by the most significant similarity.

## Summary

This chapter has continued our focus on the evaluation of evidence. We have discussed the following kinds of evidence: observation, research studies, case examples, and analogies. Each source has its strengths and weaknesses. Usually, you can rely most on those claims that writers or speakers support directly by extensive scientific research. However, many issues have not been settled by scientific research, and consequently, communicators must rely on research that is not conclusive and on other sources of evidence. You should be especially wary of claims supported by biased observation, dramatic case studies, poorly designed research, or faulty analogies. When you encounter *any* evidence, you should try to determine its quality by asking, *"How good is the evidence?"*

## Practice Exercises

[?]   *Critical Question:* **How good is the evidence?**

Evaluate each of these practice passages by examining the quality of the evidence provided.

### Passage 1

To what extent are adopted children more vulnerable to emotional and academic problems than their nonadopted peers? To answer this question, psychological and academic adjustments were evaluated in a sample of 130 adopted and 130 nonadopted children ranging in age from 6 through 11 years. Mothers and teachers rated the child's adjustment. Adoptive families were recruited from the New Jersey, Eastern Pennsylvania, and New York City areas through adoption support groups, adoptions agencies, newspaper advertisements, and word of mouth. Nonadoptive families were recruited from five central and northern New Jersey school systems and through newspaper advertisements. Adopted children were rated higher in psychological and school-related behavior problems and lower in social competence and school achievement than were nonadopted children. The results support the position that the risk of developing emotional and school-related problems is greater for adopted children.

### Passage 2

We need a system of mandatory, consistent sentences for criminals. Let's assign numbers to each criminal act based upon its severity, then assign penalties accordingly. That is the only fair way to ensure that we can get judges to dispense penalties in a just fashion. To assign a numerical value to a particular crime is not unlike equating a touchdown to six points or a field goal to three points.

Passage 3

Yes, one of the great American freedoms is our right to criticize our politicians. But we need to draw the line when freedom of speech harms our efforts to win the war against terrorists. Justice Holmes has said that yelling "Fire!" in a crowded theater creates a clear and present danger and is not protected speech. Clearly saying things that might harm the war effort creates a clear and present danger. Hasn't Holmes suggested a clear place to draw the line?

Those who argue against prohibiting such speech are in the minority. In the spring of 2002, 100 people were surveyed in at a large mall in Houston, Texas, and were asked whether they would support efforts to restrict unpatriotic anti-war speech that was going to harm the country's war effort. Eighty percent of this sample answered yes to this question.

## Sample Responses

Passage 1

CONCLUSION: *The risk of developing emotional and school-related problems is greater for adopted children.*

REASON: *Adopted children are rated higher in psychological and school-related behavior problems and lower in social competence and school achievement than are nonadopted children.*

This is just a single study, and we would want to know how typical these results are of research in this area. We also cannot tell from the information given whether the study was published in a reputable journal. However, we can ask some useful questions about the study. The sample size is quite large, but its breadth is questionable. Although multiple states were sampled, to what extent were the family sizes, family incomes, and ages of parents typical of adoptive families? Perhaps the most important sampling problem was the lack of a random sample. Given the recruiting procedures, were there selective factors that led certain kinds of parents to volunteer for the study, and were these selective procedures different for adoptive and nonadoptive families? Perhaps, for example, adoptive families are generally more willing to volunteer even if their children are experiencing problems. If such selective factors were operating, then the sample is biased.

How accurate are the rating measurements? Can parent and teacher ratings be trusted to reflect emotional adjustment accurately? How objective are parents and teachers in making their ratings? Does knowing that the child is adopted affect how one rates that child? We would want to know more about the accuracy of these ratings before we could have much confidence in the conclusion.

Passage 2

CONCLUSION: *Fixed sentences for criminals are desirable.*

REASON: *Assigning sentences for a crime is like assigning points in a football game.*

The author is trying to demonstrate a relevant similarity: assigning points to a touchdown and assigning points to a crime. Also, a system of points makes a football game fair. But, assigning points to a criminal act is a much more complex process than assigning points to a touchdown. For example, whereas we do not see the circumstances of a football touchdown as relevant to how many points we give it, we might see the circumstances of a crime as highly relevant to how much punishment a criminal should receive. Also, we may desire flexibility and a human element in the very serious business of deciding on criminal penalties, something we would not desire in a football context—a game. It is possible that judges can better determine which penalty best fits the crime because of their experience and their familiarity with the case. Because of the many relevant differences, we conclude that this analogy is not very relevant.

## CRITICAL QUESTION SUMMARY: WHY THIS QUESTION IS IMPORTANT

### How Good Is the Evidence?

When an author offers a reason in support of a conclusion, you want to know *why* you should believe that reason. By identifying the evidence offered in support of a reason, you are taking another step in evaluating the worth of the reason. If the evidence that supports the reason is good, the reason better supports the conclusion. Thus, you might be more willing to accept the author's conclusion if the author offers good evidence in support of a reason, which in turn provides good support for the conclusion.

# 10

# ARE THERE RIVAL CAUSES?

We begin this chapter with a story.

> After carefully conditioning a flea to jump out of a box following the presentation of a loud noise, the researcher removed the first pair of legs to see what effect this had. Observing that the flea was still able to perform his task, the scientist removed the second pair of legs. Once again noting no difference in performance, the researcher removed the final pair of legs and found that the jumping behavior no longer occurred. Thus, the investigator wrote in his notebook, "When all the legs of a flea have been removed, it will no longer be able to hear."[1]

This story clearly illustrates a common goal in the use of evidence: answering the question, "What *caused* something to happen?" For example, what caused the murder rate to decrease in the United States in 2000? Or, *why* has the rate of depression among teenagers increased over the last 10 years?

The story also shows a very common difficulty in using evidence to prove that something caused something else—the problem of *rival causes*. The above fictional researcher offered one interpretation of his research findings: removal of the legs affected the flea's ability to hear. We expect that you can see that there is another very plausible interpretation for why the flea stopped jumping.

---

[1] Adapted from Schuyler W. Huck and Howard M. Sandler, *Rival Hypotheses* (New York: Harper & Row, 1979), p. xiii.

Thus, this story shows that the *same evidence* can be consistent with *different* interpretations. We refer to those different interpretations as rival causes. As we use the term, *rival cause* implies some alternative interpretation, different from the interpretation made by the communicator, for why events turned out as they did.

Although rival causes will rarely be as obvious as they are in our story, you will frequently encounter experts presenting one hypothesis to explain events or research findings when other plausible hypotheses could also explain them. Usually, these experts will not reveal rival causes to you; you will have to produce them. Doing so can be especially helpful as you decide "how good is the evidence?" because the existence of multiple, plausible rival causes for events reduces our confidence in the cause originally offered by the author.

Searching for rival causes will always be appropriate when a speaker or writer presents you with some evidence and offers a cause to explain it.

[?]    *Critical Question: **Are there rival causes?***

**Attention:**   A rival cause is a plausible interpretation, different from one author's interpretation, that can explain why a certain outcome occurred.

## When to Look for Rival Causes

You need to look for rival causes when you have good reason to believe that the writer or speaker is using evidence to support a claim about the cause of something. The word *cause* means "to bring about, make happen, or affect." Communicators can indicate causal thinking to you in a number of ways. We have listed a few.

| | |
|---|---|
| X has the effect of . . . | X deters . . . |
| X facilitates . . . | as a result of X . . . |
| X leads to . . . | X increases the likelihood . . . |
| X influences . . . | X determines . . . |
| X is a factor in . . . | X contributes to . . . |
| X is linked to . . . | X is related to . . . |
| X is associated with . . . | |

These clues to causal thinking should help you recognize when a communicator is making a causal claim. Once you note such a claim, be alert to the possibility of rival causes.

## The Pervasiveness of Rival Causes

On Sunday evening, December 23, 1888, Vincent van Gogh, then 35 years old, cut off the lower half of his left ear and took it to a brothel, where he asked for a prostitute named Rachel and handed the ear to her, requesting that she "keep this object carefully."

Authors have offered numerous hypotheses to explain this event, including the following:

1. He was frustrated by two recent events: the engagement of his brother Theo, to whom he was very attached, and the failure of an attempt to establish a working and living relationship with Paul Gauguin. The aggressive impulses aroused by these frustrations were first directed at Gauguin, but then were turned against himself.[2]

2. Van Gogh had a great sympathy for prostitutes and identified with their status as social outcasts. One suggestion is that his self-mutilation was a reflection of this identification. "In June, just a few months before butchering his ear, he had written that 'the whore is like meat in a butcher shop'; when he treated his own body as 'meat in a butcher's shop,' he reversed their roles, identified himself with the whore, and showed his sympathy for her."[3]

3. It is likely that van Gogh experienced frightening auditory hallucinations during his psychotic attack similar to those that he experienced in other attacks. Afterward, while in the sanitarium, he wrote that other patients heard strange sounds and voices as he had and speculated in one case that this was probably due to a disease of nerves in the ear. Thus, in a psychotic state, van Gogh could have felt that his own ear was diseased and cut it off to silence the disturbing sounds.[4]

The case of van Gogh and the missing ear has recently taken a turn that often happens in searches for causes. A rival cause that no one had considered

---

[2] William M. Runyan, *Life Histories and Psychobiography* (New York: Oxford University Press, 1982): 38–39.

[3] Ibid., p. 40.

[4] Ibid., pp. 40–41.

turns out to be the most likely candidate. Recent evidence suggests that van Gogh was actually suffering from an inner-ear infection and that he cut off his ear to ease the excruciating pain.

Now, let's leave van Gogh's case for a moment and examine a different event in need of explanation—the findings of a research study.

> A researcher reported that treating headaches with relaxation exercises and biofeedback is helpful. Three-fourths of 95 people with chronic tension headaches and about half of 75 migraine sufferers studied reduced the frequency and severity of their headaches after learning how to relax head, neck, and shoulder muscles and control stress and tension with biofeedback.

In this study, the researcher probably began with the hypothesis that relaxation training *causes* reduction of headache suffering; and he found evidence consistent with that hypothesis. But let us offer several rival, or different, causes for the same findings.

1.  Research participants were highly suggestible, and the *expectation of improvement* was responsible for the change; like the sugar pill placebo effect in medicine, thinking they were going to get better might have stimulated a number of physical and mental processes that caused participants to feel better.

2.  Participants wanted to please the researchers; thus, they reported feeling better even though they did not.

3.  Most participants volunteered while undergoing highly stressful life situations; they experienced a reduction in life stress during the course of the study; and this reduction accounted for the reduction in symptoms.

Now, let's leave the research laboratory for a moment and move to the health pages of our newspapers and examine an argument related to health-care statistics.

> In the year 2000, healthcare costs increased 7.2 percent, the largest jump in a decade. Hospitals need to curtail the rising use of very expensive high-tech diagnostic and treatment procedures, such as organ transplants and Magnetic Resonance Imaging.

The hypothesis offered by the writer is that hospital's excessive use of high-tech procedures is causing the rising cost of healthcare. But, let's again generate some plausible rival causes:

1. Our population is aging; medical costs rise because in general an aging population uses more healthcare services than a younger one.

2. Patients are suing increasing numbers of doctors for very large sums of money and paying attorneys very large contingency fees; this trend is causing insurance companies to increase their rates for physicians, which in turn causes physicians to charge more for their services.

3. The prices of prescription drugs have gone up dramatically, and patients are becoming increasingly dependent on drugs for treatment of minor ailments.

Now, let's examine some important lessons that can be learned from the van Gogh case, the research study, and the healthcare statistics.

---

## Lessons Learned

1. Many kinds of events are open to explanation by rival causes, including clinical case studies, criminal trials, research studies, stock market trends, advertising statistics, sports page charts, airline crash findings, and historical events.

2. Experts can examine the same evidence and come up with different causes to explain it.

3. Although many explanations can "fit the facts," some seem *more plausible* than others.

4. Most communicators will provide you with only their favored causes; the critical reader or listener must generate rival causes.

5. Generating rival causes is a creative process; usually such causes will not be obvious.

6. Even "scientific" researchers frequently fail to acknowledge important rival causes for their findings.

7. Finally, the certainty of a particular causal claim is inversely related to the number of plausible rival causes.

In the following sections, we explore the implications of these lessons for the critical thinker.

## Detecting Rival Causes

Locating rival causes is much like being a good detective. When you recognize situations in which rival causes are possible, you want to ask yourself questions like:

---

? Can I think of any other way to interpret the evidence?

? What else might have caused this act or these findings?

? If I looked at this from another point of view, what might I see as important causes?

? If this interpretation is incorrect, what other interpretation might make sense?

---

As you search for rival causes, try to *blind yourself to the author's interpretation and see whether you can construct your own.*

## *The* Cause or *A* Cause

A mass murder occurs in a school. Talk show hosts begin to interview the experts about *the* cause. It's guns. It's parental neglect. It's TV violence. It's lack of religion. It's stress. The experts may *claim* to have the answer, but they are not likely to *know* it. That is because a frequently made error is to look for a simple, single cause of an event when it is really the result of a combination of many *contributory* causes—a cause that helps to create a total set of conditions necessary for the event to occur.

Multiple contributory causes occur more often than do single causes in situations involving the characteristics or activities of humans. In many cases, the best causal explanation is one that combines a considerable number of causes that *only together* are sufficient to bring about the event. So, the best answer experts can give to the talk show hosts' question is "We don't know *the* cause for such events, but we can speculate about possible causes that might have contributed to the event." Thus, when we are searching for rival causes, we need to remember that any single cause that we identify is much more likely to be a contributory cause than *the* cause.

When communicators fail to consider the complexity of causes, they commit the following reasoning fallacy:

---

F: **Causal Oversimplification:**    Explaining an event by relying on causal factors that are insufficient to account for the event or by overemphasizing the role of one or more of these factors.

---

In some sense, almost all causal explanations are oversimplifications; thus you want to be fair to communicators who offer explanations that do not include *every* possible cause of an event. Causal conclusions, however, should include sufficient causal factors to convince you that they are not too greatly oversimplified, or the author should make clear to you that the causal factor he emphasizes in his conclusion is only one of a number of possible contributing causes—**a** cause, not **the** cause.

## Rival Causes and Scientific Research

Scientific research attempts to isolate some of the most important contributing causes from other extraneous causes and provides a major source of hypotheses about what causes events in our world. Researchers start with tentative beliefs—hypotheses—about causes of events. For example, researchers generated many hypotheses about the cause of AIDS. One hypothesis was that AIDS is caused by a virus. Once a hypothesis has been firmly established by dependable research evidence, it changes from a hypothesis to a law. In the domain of complex human behavior, however, there are very few established general laws. Stated claims like "TV violence causes crime," and "child-centered parenting causes emotional security in adults" sound like laws, but we need to remain skeptical of the generalizability of such claims. They must currently be viewed as hypotheses, not laws, and are best stated as follows: "TV violence may be a contributing cause to certain kinds of crime," and "child-centered parenting may be a contributing cause to emotional security in adults."

Then, what should you do when speakers or writers use findings from research studies to conclude that one event causes another? First, remember that their conclusion should be viewed as **a** cause, not **the** cause. Then try to find out as much as you can about the research procedures used to produce the findings that support the hypothesis. Finally, try to determine rival causes that might explain the findings. The more plausible rival causes that can account for the findings, the less faith you should have in the hypothesis favored by the communicator.

Because a major goal of scientific research is to minimize the number of plausible hypotheses for research findings, scientists have devised many techniques for ruling out, or eliminating, plausible rival causes. Sometimes these techniques work very well, and only a single hypothesis seems justifiably supported by the evidence. In such cases we can have some confidence in the dependability of that hypothesis. However, much research fails to sufficiently rule out important rival causes, especially research that studies complex human behavior.

Let's use the following argument to practice detecting rival causes.

> Taking daily doses of vitamin E appears to cut the risk of heart disease between one-third and one-half, a major new study concludes. The results strengthen the newly popular belief that vitamins and other so-called antioxidants are good for the heart. Research findings were from the Nurses' Health Study, which enrolled 87,245 female nurses from across the United States. Seventeen percent of the nurses took vitamin E. During eight years of follow-up, 552 women suffered heart attacks. The researchers found that women who had taken vitamin E for more than two years had a 46 percent lower risk of a heart attack.

Should you rush out and buy vitamin E supplements? Not until you consider rival causes! How else might one explain these group differences?

First, let's outline the reasoning:

CONCLUSION: (Researchers' hypothesis) *Taking daily doses of vitamin E appears to cut the risk of heart disease between one-third and one-half.*

REASON: (Researchers' evidence) *Research study showed women who had taken vitamin E had a lower risk of heart attack than those who had not.*

Note that the words *appears to cut* in the conclusion tell us the researchers are making a causal claim about the evidence. But other hypotheses can explain this evidence.

The report fails to tell us why particular women took vitamin E. Isn't it possible that nurses who take vitamin E are the type of people who tend to maintain good health habits, such as exercising frequently and not eating fatty foods? If so, differences in exercise and eating habits are a plausible rival hypothesis that could explain the differences in heart attack risk between the two groups. Also, the women using vitamin E may be wealthier than the others and thus perhaps face a lower level of general life stress. We bet you can think of other reasons these two groups—vitamin E users and nonusers—differ in their risk of heart disease.

We cannot make you aware of all possible rival causes. In the following selections, however, we provide several clues for finding common rival causes.

## Rival Causes for Differences Between Groups

One of the most common ways for researchers to try to find a cause for some event is to *compare groups*. For example, you will frequently encounter the following kinds of references to group comparisons:

> Researchers compared an experimental group to a control group.
>
> One group received treatment X; the other group didn't.
>
> A group with clogged arteries was compared with a group without clogged arteries.

When researchers find differences between groups, they often conclude, "Those differences support our hypothesis." For example, a researcher might compare a group of cancer patients treated with a new drug with a control group of cancer patients that does not get the new drug, find that the groups differ in their recovery from cancer, and then conclude that the drug caused the difference. The problem is that *research groups almost always differ in more than one important way,* and thus group differences often are consistent with multiple causes. Thus, when you see communicators use findings of differences between groups to support one cause, always ask, "Are there rival causes that might also explain the differences in the groups?"

Let's take a look at a study that compares groups and try to detect rival causes.

> In a recent research study, Teacher A's teaching method for a psychology course was judged superior to that of Teacher B for that same course because Teacher A's class performed much better, on the average, than Teacher B's class on the same standardized, final, comprehensive multiple-choice test.

Here we have two groups: the classes of Teacher A and Teacher B. The question we need to ask is, "Did these two groups differ in important ways other than the teaching they experienced?" Did you think of either of the following possible important differences between the two groups that might account for test score differences?

- *Differences in students' average intelligence.* It is possible that, on the average, more intelligent students signed up for Teacher A than for Teacher B, perhaps because they heard Teacher A was more challenging.
- *Differences in motivation.* Perhaps one class was taught earlier in the day than another. Students who sign up for a class taught early in the day may be more motivated to learn than students who sign up for a class which is taught later in the day. Or perhaps the personalities of the two instructors differed greatly, influencing the motivation of the students.

You probably came up with other important differences. Remember: *Many factors can cause research groups to differ!*

## Confusing Causation with Association

We have an inherent tendency to "see" events that are associated, or that "go together," as events that cause one another. That is, we conclude that because characteristic X (e.g., amount of TV viewing) is associated with characteristic Y (e.g., performance in school), that X therefore causes Y. The following are examples of such reasoning:

1. States with low speed limits tend to have a lower rate of highway death than states with higher speed limits; thus, low speed limits deter highway deaths.
2. Absence of a father in the home occurs at a higher rate with juvenile delinquents than with nondelinquents; thus, father absence is a cause of juvenile delinquency.

When we think this way, we are, however, often very wrong! Why? Usually, because multiple hypotheses can explain why X and Y "go together." In fact, there are at least four different kinds of hypotheses to account for any such relationship. Knowing what these are will help you discover rival causes. Let's illustrate each of the four with a research example.

A recent study reported that "hostility hurts women's health." The researchers studied 102 women over a 31-year period and found that women high in hostility at ages 21, 27, and 43 had more sickness at 52 than women low in hostility. "That includes everything from colds to serious illness." The researchers hypothesize that anger may release stress hormones or impair immunity.

Should women with a high degree of hostility be worried about their physical health? Not yet. Before they do, they should contemplate each of four potential explanations for the research findings.

Explanation 1: *X is a cause of Y.* (Hostility does indeed impair women's health.)

Explanation 2: *Y is a cause of X.* (Being in poor health may make women feel hostile.)

Explanation 3: *X and Y are associated because of some third factor, Z.* (Perhaps both hostility and poor health are caused by poor-health-related behaviors, such as smoking and lack of exercise, or perhaps by stressful life events.)

Explanation 4: *X and Y influence each other.* (Perhaps feeling hostile weakens one's immune system, and in turn, a weaker immune system makes one feel tired, and this makes one feel more hostile.)

*Remember: Association or correlation does not prove causation!*

Yet much evidence to prove causation is only based on association or correlation. When an author supports a hypothesis by pointing to an association between characteristics, always ask, "Are there other causes that explain the association?"

Test yourself on the following:

A recent study reported that baldness is correlated with heart attack risk; baldheaded people have a higher risk of dying of an early heart attack than non-baldheaded people.

We hope you can now see that baldheaded people might be ill-advised to buy the newest hair-growing lotion to prevent a heart attack. What rival causes did you think of? Couldn't poor blood circulation or genetic inheritance account for the association between baldheadedness (X) and bad hearts (Y)?

This confusion between correlation and causation is as understandable as it is dangerous. A cause will indeed precede its effect. But many things preceded that effect. Most of them were not causal.

You should now be able to identify two common causal reasoning fallacies by attending to the above four possible explanations of why events might be associated:

---

F: **Confusion of Cause and Effect:** Confusing the cause with the effect of an event or failing to recognize that the two events may be influencing each other.

---

---

F: **Neglect of a Common Cause:**    Failure to recognize that two events may be related because of the effects of a common third factor.

---

## Strong Support for a Cause

In your hunt for rival causes, it should be helpful for you to know when scientific research provides good support for a particular cause. Although this is a very complex question, which you should pursue in more depth elsewhere, here are a few "rules of thumb" that should be helpful to you.

- The researcher doesn't have any personal financial incentive in suggesting the cause.
- The research had at least one control group, such as a group that did not get exposed to the cause.
- Groups that were compared differed on very few characteristics other than the causal factor of interest.
- Research participants were randomly assigned to groups; they did not get to select which group they were in.
- Participants were unaware of the researchers' hypotheses.
- Other researchers have replicated the findings.

## Confusing "After this" with "Because of this"

Shortly after George W. Bush became president, the stock market sharply dropped in value. Can we conclude that the Bush presidency caused this drop? No. There are many other possible causes. If we were to infer such a conclusion, we would be illustrating a very common way that people confuse causation with association.

Often, we try to explain a particular event as follows: Because event B *followed* event A, then event A *caused* event B. Such reasoning occurs because human beings have a strong tendency to believe that if two events occur close together in time, the first one must have caused the second one.

To appreciate the flaw in this reasoning, pick up today's newspaper and make a list of what is going on in the world. Then pick up yesterday's newspaper and make a similar list. Could you conclude that the events of yesterday are causing the events of today? Clearly not. For example, yesterday's news reported that *Lord of the Rings: The Fellowship of the Rings* broke attendance records for movies, and today's news reported that a major airline was approaching bankruptcy. It is highly unlikely that excitement about *Lord of the Rings* caused the airline's financial problems. Many events that occur after other events in time are not caused by the preceding events. When we wrongly conclude that the first event causes the second because it preceded it, we commit the *Post hoc, ergo propter hoc* (meaning: "after this, therefore because of this") fallacy, or, for short, the Post hoc fallacy. Such reasoning is responsible for many superstitious beliefs. For example, you may have done very well on a test just after eating a particular cereal; now, you eat that cereal before every test.

---

F: **Post hoc Fallacy:**    Assuming that a particular event, B, is caused by another event, A, simply because B follows A in time.

---

The following examples further illustrate the problem with this kind of reasoning.

> "Harry Hurricane must be an excellent coach; since he moved to our university, the team's record has improved dramatically." (But maybe the university also decided to double its athletic budget when Harry came.)

> "Since the Supreme Court decisions granting the accused more rights, the crime rate has steadily increased." (But maybe increases in unemployment have also occurred since those Supreme Court decisions.)

As you might guess, political and business leaders are fond of using the Post hoc argument, especially when it works in their favor. For example, they tend to take credit for anything good that takes place after they assumed their leadership role and to place blame elsewhere for anything bad that happens.

*Remember:* The finding that one event follows another in time does not by itself prove causation; it may be only a coincidence. When you see such reasoning, always ask yourself, "Are there rival causes that could account for the event?" and, "Is there any good evidence other than the fact that one event followed the other event in time?"

## Explaining Individual Events or Acts

Why did executives of a very large energy company deceive its stockholders in 2002? Why did terrorists attack the World Trade Center on September 11, 2001? What caused the drought in the Southwest in 2002?

Like our question about van Gogh's ear, these questions seek explanations of individual historical events. Scientific research studies cannot answer the questions. Instead, we must search the past for clues. Such a search makes us highly susceptible to reasoning errors for several reasons. A few of these are especially important to remember.

First, as we saw in the van Gogh case, so many different stories for the same event can "make sense." Second, the way we explain events is greatly influenced by social and political forces, as well as by individual psychological forces. For example, "liberals" might view the causes of executive misbehavior differently from "conservatives," and feminists might view the causes of anorexia much differently from physicians.

Also, a common bias is "the *fundamental attribution error*," in which we typically overestimate the importance of personal tendencies relative to situational factors in interpreting the behavior of others. That is, we tend to see the cause of other's behavior as coming from within (their personal characteristics) rather than from without (situational forces.) So, for example, when someone shows up late for a date, we're likely to view the lateness initially as a result of a tendency of the person to procrastinate or to be inconsiderate. However, we should also consider the role of unforeseen circumstances, such as car trouble, heavy traffic, or unanticipated company.

Another kind of common psychological error is to start with a limited number of possible causes and then to interpret additional information (even if it is irrelevant) as corroborating these existing hypotheses, rather than keeping the information separate or generating new, perhaps more complex, hypotheses. Our tendency is to simplify the world; yet often explanations require much complexity. Explaining events is not as simple as frequently portrayed by guest experts on the popular talk shows.

How can we know whether we have a "good" explanation of a particular event or set of events? We can never know for sure. But we can make some progress by asking critical questions.

Be wary of accepting the first interpretation of an event you encounter. Search for rival causes and try to compare their credibility. We must accept the fact that *many* events do not have a simple explanation.

---

### Clues for Explaining an Event or Set of Events

Ask yourself the following questions when trying to generate rival causes for events.

? Is there any evidence that the explanation has been critically examined?

? Is it likely that social, political, or psychological forces may bias the hypothesis?

? What *rival causes* have not been considered? How credible is the author's hypothesis compared to rival causes?

? Is the hypothesis *thorough* in accounting for many puzzling aspects of the events in question?

? How *consistent* is the hypothesis with all the available valuable relevant evidence?

? Is the Post hoc fallacy the primary reasoning being used to link the events?

---

## Evaluating Rival Causes

The more plausible the rival causes that you come up with, the less faith you can have in the initial explanation offered, at least until further evidence has been considered. As a critical thinker, you will want to assess as best you can how each of the alternative explanations fits the available evidence, trying to be sensitive to your personal biases.

In comparing causes, we suggest that you apply the following criteria:

1. their logical soundness,
2. their consistency with other knowledge that you have, and
3. their previous success in explaining or predicting events.

## USING THIS CRITICAL QUESTION

Every assertion about causation should trigger immediate curiosity in the mind of a critical thinker. But are there alternative causes for the phenomenon? Asking someone to consider rival causes is constructive criticism at its finest. Your objective in doing so is to find a better causal explanation.

## Evidence and Your Own Writing and Speaking

The last three chapters have indirectly provided you with a clue for effective communication. Your audience will be justifiably impressed when you provide strong and sufficient evidence for your claims. But implicit in this clue is a warning: Your audience expects and should demand that your claims are supported by thorough evidence. Satisfying this demand is one of your greatest challenges as a writer and speaker.

## Summary

Factual claims about the causes of events are weakened when other claims about the causes can be offered. Such claims are *rival causes*.

A common logical error in explaining observations is to confuse causation with association. Thus, always ask what other causes might explain observed associations. Be especially alert to the Post hoc fallacy.

 *Critical Question:* **Are there rival causes?**

## Practice Exercises

Each of the following examples provides an argument to support a causal claim. Try to generate rival causes for such claims. Then try to determine how much you have weakened the author's claim by knowledge of rival causes.

Passage 1

A little bit of light may beat the winter blues. Researchers studied nine patients who suffered from winter depression, which is caused when the days get shorter. The patients were exposed to bright fluorescent light upon awakening and in the late afternoon, for three hours at a time. Within a week, seven of the patients had recovered from their depression completely, and the other two showed a modest improvement. The light treatment works because it tricks the body into thinking that it's summer.

Passage 2

Why did the postal worker go berserk and kill those six employees? The answer is provided by a close look at his childhood. He lost his mother when he was 8, and his father often physically abused him. Also, he grew up in the shadow of more successful older siblings. As a child he had a difficult time making friends and had trouble establishing a sexual identity. Then, as an adult he drifted from job to job, while developing increasingly bizarre fantasies. Eventually, the post office became a symbol of the society that had caused his failures. To become "somebody," he ultimately turned to violence.

Passage 3

According to a recent study, one of the major causes of delinquent behavior during teenage years is low self-esteem in adolescents. Researchers studied over 500 children from the Nashville, Tennessee Adolescent Potential study, which has been examining the causes of delinquent behavior. The adolescents in the study were interviewed while in the ninth grade. They completed the McRoberts Self-Esteem test, and then were asked how often they participated in various kinds of crimes. The researchers found that the worse the kids felt about themselves, the more likely they were to engage in delinquent acts. Also, the researchers found that the children whose self-esteem scores increased over the next two years also tended to show a decrease in delinquent behavior. Such research shows the need for teachers to attend to an adolescents' self-esteem if they are to reduce the amount of juvenile crime.

## Sample Responses

Passage 1

CONCLUSION: *Light treatment combats winter depression.*

REASONS: *Seven of nine patients exposed to light treatment completely recovered from their depression in a week's time.*

Can anything else account for the change besides light treatment? Yes; the researcher fails to rule out many obvious alternative explanations. For example, the patients might have *expected* to get better, and these *expectancies* might have led to feeling better. Also, they knew the purpose of the light treatment, and a rival cause is that they *tried to please* the researchers by reporting that they felt better. We can also hypothesize that external events during the one-week treatment period caused the change. Perhaps during the week of treatment, for example, the weather was especially good, and these people spent much more time exercising outside than usual. Another possibility is that these people were suffering from a form of depression from which they could naturally expect to recover in a short period of time. Can you locate other rival causes?

Passage 2

CONCLUSION:    *The violent act of killing the post office workers was caused by experiencing a broken home, physical abuse, sibling rivalry, and loneliness in childhood.*

REASON:    *The killer's childhood had these characteristics.*

It is possible that these childhood factors were important determinants of the acts of violence. But most people who have suffered such childhoods do not commit violent acts. Are there other possible causes for such behavior? As in the case of van Gogh, we suspect there may be many other plausible explanations. Before we could conclude that these childhood events were the causal factors, we would want to know more about this childhood and more about recent events in his life. For example, had he suffered any recent head injuries? Had he been using drugs? Had he had any recent highly stressful experiences with co-workers? After the fact, we can always find childhood experiences that make sense as causes of adult behavior. Before we draw causal conclusions, however, we must seek more evidence to prove that the one set of events caused the other than the mere fact that one set of events preceded the other set.

 ## CRITICAL QUESTION SUMMARY: WHY THIS QUESTION IS IMPORTANT

### Are There Rival Causes?

While an author might offer an explanation for why certain events occurred, other explanations might be plausible. When you try to identify rival causes, you are finding alternative explanations for an event. If you can identify alternative explanations, you must decide whether you should believe the author's explanation or one of the other explanations. If the author does not provide reasons for why you should accept his explanation over other explanations, you should not be willing to accept his explanation and, ultimately, his conclusion. Thus, looking for rival causes is another step in deciding whether to accept or reject an argument.

# ARE THE STATISTICS
# DECEPTIVE?

How much should you be persuaded by the following passages?

> The National Coalition Against Domestic Violence estimates that more than half of married women (more than 27 million) will experience violence during their marriage, and that more than one-third (more than 18 million) are battered repeatedly every year.

> Women are better drivers than men, as proven by the fact that of men involved in accidents, 23 percent had been drinking—compared to 9.6 percent of the women.

You should not be very impressed by the above reasoning. Both arguments *deceive us with statistics!*

One of the most frequent kinds of evidence that authors present is "statistics." You have probably often heard people use the following phrase to help support their argument: "I have statistics to prove it." We use statistics (often inappropriately) to assess our nation's economic activity, to determine which TV shows will survive, to determine investment strategy, to help people decide on which sports teams to bet, to assess the country's social progress, to evaluate our sexual satisfaction, to predict the weather, and to provide input for many other issues.

Statistics are evidence expressed as numbers. Such evidence can seem quite impressive because numbers make evidence appear to be very scientific and precise, as though it represents "the facts." Statistics, however, can, and often do, lie! They do not necessarily prove what they appear to prove.

As a critical thinker, you should strive to detect erroneous statistical reasoning. In a few short paragraphs, we cannot show you all the different ways that people can "lie with statistics." However, this chapter will provide some general strategies that you can use to detect such deception. In addition, it will alert you to flaws in statistical reasoning by illustrating a number of the most common ways that authors misuse statistical evidence.

 *Critical Question: **Are the statistics deceptive?***

## Unknowable and Biased Statistics

The first strategy for locating deceptive statistics is to try to find out as much as you can about how the statistics were obtained. Can we know precisely the number of people in the United States who have AIDS, have abortions, shoplift, commit white-collar crimes, engage in affairs, drink more than three beers a day, beat their wives, are homeless, or use cocaine? We suspect not. Why? Because there are a variety of obstacles to getting accurate statistics for certain purposes, including unwillingness to provide truthful information, failure to report events, and physical barriers to observing events. Consequently, statistics are often in the form of "educated guesses." Such estimates can be quite useful; they can also be quite deceiving. Always ask, "How did the author arrive at the estimate?"

One common place to find such errors is in reports of the incidence of various physical and medical disorders, especially when there is an effort to solicit attention to the disorder. For example, a recent book on eating disorders stated that every year 150,000 young women die of anorexia nervosa; the media picked up this number and cited it frequently. Others, alarmed by the frequency, took a closer look and found that 150,000 women *suffered* from eating disorders, but only 54 died in a recent year. These examples remind us to be wary of impressive or alarming numbers that are being used to persuade us, especially when it is highly unlikely that a precise measurement would be possible in the first place.

## Confusing Averages

Examine the following statements:

(1) Americans are better off than ever; the average salary of an American worker is now $35,000.

(2) The average pollution of air by factories is now well below the dangerous level.

Both examples use the word "average." But there are three different ways to determine an average, and in most cases each will give you a different average. What are the three ways? One is to add all the values and divide this total by the number of values used. The result is the mean.

A second way is to list all the values from highest to lowest, then find the one in the middle. This middle value is the median. Half of the values will be above the median; half will be below it. A third way is to list all the values and then count each different value or range of values. The value that appears most frequently is called the mode, the third kind of average.

It makes a big difference whether a writer is talking about the mean, median, or mode. Think about the salary distribution in the United States. Some individuals are paid extremely high salaries, such as $2,000,000 per year. Such high salaries will increase the mean dramatically. They will have little effect, however, on either the median or the mode. Thus, if one wishes to make the average salary seem high, the mean is probably the best average to present. You should now be able to see how important it is to know which average is used when people talk about salaries or income.

Now, let's look carefully at example (2). If the average presented is either the mode or the median, we may be tricked into a false sense of security. For example, what if only a few factories pollute highly, but the amount they pollute is far above the dangerous level—so far above that the air as a whole is still being dangerously polluted. In such a case, the mode and the median pollution values could be quite low, but the mean would be very high.

When you see "average" values, always ask: "Does it matter whether it is the mean, the median, or the mode?" To answer this question, consider how using the various meanings of average might change the significance of the information.

Not only is it important to determine whether an average is a mean, median, or mode, but it is often also important to determine the gap between the smallest and largest values—the range—and how frequently each of the values occurs—the distribution. For example, assume that you have to make the decision about whether to eat some fish caught in a nearby ocean. Would you be satisfied with information about the average mercury content in those fish? We wouldn't.

We would want to know the range of mercury content, in other words, the highest and lowest levels possible as well as the frequency of the different levels. The average may be in the "safe" level; but if 10 percent of the fish contained levels of mercury well above the "safe" level, we suspect that you would rather eat something else for supper.

Let's consider another example in which knowing the range and distribution would be important.

America is not overcrowded. Nationally we have fewer than 60 people per square mile, a population density lower than that of most other countries.

First, we suspect that this population density figure represents the mean. While the mean density may be quite low, there obviously are areas in the United States, in the Northeast, for example, with very high-density figures. Thus, America may indeed be overcrowded in some areas, even though on the average it is not.

Thus, when an average is presented, ask yourself: "Would it be important for me to know the range and distribution of values?"

## Concluding One Thing, Proving Another

Communicators often deceive us when they use statistics that prove one thing but then claim to have proved something quite different. The statistics don't prove what they seem to! We suggest two strategies for locating such deception.

One strategy is to *blind yourself to the communicator's statistics* and ask yourself, "What statistical evidence would be helpful in proving her conclusion?" Then, compare the needed statistics to the statistics given. If the two do not match, you may have located a statistical deception. The following example provides you with an opportunity to apply that strategy.

A car dealer raved that a particular car was a big success because only 5 out of 100 buyers who bought the car had complained to the dealership about its performance. "When 95 percent of buyers are pleased," the salesman was heard to say, "then that's a darn good car."

How should the car dealer have proven his conclusion that 95 percent of buyers are pleased? Shouldn't he have randomly sampled a large number of buyers from among all buyers of that particular car and asked them, "Are you pleased with your car?" Instead, he has heard only from those who complained and then assumed that all noncomplainers were pleased with the car, an unwarranted assumption. The dealer thus proves one thing (few buyers complained) and concludes another (most buyers were pleased). An important lesson to learn from this example is to *pay close attention to both the wording of the statistics and the wording of the conclusion* to see whether they are referring to the same thing. When they are not, the author or speaker may be lying with statistics.

It is frequently difficult to know just what statistical evidence should be provided to back up a conclusion. Thus, let us suggest a further strategy. Examine the author's statistics *very closely* while *blinding yourself to the conclusion;*

then ask yourself, "What is the appropriate conclusion to be drawn from those statistics?" Then, compare your conclusion with the author's. Try that strategy with the following example.

> Almost one-fourth of psychotherapists have sexually abused patients who were minors. A clinical psychologist surveyed distinguished psychologists around the country. Of the 90 who replied to the survey, 24 percent said they knew of instances in which therapists abused minor patients.

Did you come up with the following conclusion? Almost one-fourth of therapists *claim to know about* instances when therapists abused minor patients. Do you see the difference between what the statistics proved and what the author concluded? If so, you have discovered how this author has lied with statistics.

Now, practice on the following.

> In 1995, a newspaper columnist asked female readers, "Would you be content to be held close and treated tenderly and forget about 'the act'?" She reported that 72 percent of the respondents answered "yes" and concluded, "The survey means that a tremendous number of women out there are not enjoying sex."

Do you see how the writer has concluded one thing while proving another? Do you think results might have been different if the columnist had asked, "Are you enjoying sexual activity?"

## Deceiving by Omitting Information

Statistics often deceive us because they are incomplete. Thus, a further helpful strategy for locating flaws in statistical reasoning is to ask, *"What further information do you need before you can judge the impact of the statistics?"* Let's look at two examples to illustrate the usefulness of this question.

1.  A crime wave has hit our city. Homicides have increased by 67 percent in the last year.
2.  Boxing is less dangerous than other contact sports. A survey of sports-related deaths in New York City over a 30-year period revealed that baseball, with 43 deaths, led both football (22) and boxing (21) in terms of mortality.

At first, 67 percent seems quite impressive. But something is missing: the absolute numbers on which this percentage is based. Wouldn't we be less alarmed if we knew that this increase was from three homicides to five, rather than from 300 to 500? In our second example, we have the numbers, but we don't have the percentages. Wouldn't we need to know what these numbers mean in terms of percentages of athletes involved in the sports? After all, there are fewer total boxers than there are baseball players.

When you encounter impressive-sounding numbers or percentages, be wary. You may need to get other information to decide just how impressive the numbers are.

Another important kind of potential missing information is *relevant comparisons*. It is often useful to ask the question, "As compared to . . . ?"

Each of the following statements illustrates statistics that can benefit from asking for comparisons:

1. Fizz aspirin works 50 percent faster.
2. Funding for AIDS research is more than adequate. Last year the government spent over $1.2 billion on AIDS research.
3. College degrees pay off. A recent survey found that workers with a bachelor's degree were earning an average of $35,000 per year in the spring of 2000.

With reference to the first statement, don't you need to ask, "Fifty percent faster than what?" Other ineffective aspirins? Previous Fizz aspirin? As for the second statement, wouldn't you want to ask how the expenditure compares to previous years, or to research on other diseases, or to the total spent by the government on health-related research? With reference to the third statement, how does that average compare to the average earnings of equally intelligent people who decided not to go to college?

When you encounter statistics, be sure to ask, "What relevant information is missing?"

## Risk Statistics and Omitted Information

"Drug X will reduce your risk of colon cancer by 5 percent."

"Studies show that mammograms as screening devices for 50-year-old women can reduce breast cancer deaths by 10 percent."

A common use of statistics in arguments—especially arguments about health risks—is the reporting of risk reduction as a result of some intervention. Such reports can be deceptive. The same amount of risk reduction can be reported in *relative* or *absolute* terms, and these differences can greatly affect our perceptions of the actual amount of risk reduction.

Imagine a 60-year-old man with heart problems discussing with his doctor the potential benefits of available treatments to help prevent a future heart attack. The doctor quotes statistics about three treatment options:

(1) Treatment X will reduce the likelihood of a heart attack by 20 percent,

(2) Treatment Y will reduce the risk by 1 percent, and

(3) With treatment Z, 96 percent of men are free of heart attacks for 5 years, compared to 95 percent of those who go untreated.

Which treatment should he choose? Our guess is that he will choose the first. But all of these options refer to the same size treatment effect. They just express the risk in different ways. The first (the 20 percent) is the "relative risk reduction." If a treatment reduces the risk of heart attack from 5 in 100 to 4 in 100, the risk is reduced by 1/5, or 20 percent. But the *absolute* change, from 5 to 4 percent, is only a 1 percent reduction, and the improvement of a good outcome from 95 to 96 is also only 1 percent. The point is that expressing risk reductions in relative, rather than absolute terms, can make treatment effects seem larger than they really are, and individuals are more likely to embrace a treatment when benefits are expressed in relative rather than absolute terms. As you might expect, drug companies usually use relative risk in their ads, and media reports also tend to focus on relative risk.

Relative risk reduction statistics can be deceiving. When you encounter arguments using such statistics, always try to determine how the results might be different and less impressive if expressed in absolute terms.

## Summary

We have highlighted a number of ways by which you can catch people "lying" with statistics. We hope that you can now see the problems with statistics on domestic violence and on driving ability that we presented at the beginning of the chapter. *Hints:* Where did that impressive figure of more than 27 million come from? If you were to use statistics to compare male and female driving ability, wouldn't you be primarily interested in the number of accidents per mile driven, rather than in the statistics provided?

---

### Clues for Assessing Statistics

1.  Try to find out as much as you can about how the statistics were obtained. Ask, *"How does the author or speaker know?"*

2.  Be curious about the type of average being described.

3.  Be alert to users of statistics *concluding one thing, but proving another.*

4.  Blind yourself to the writer's or speaker's statistics and compare the needed statistical evidence with the statistics actually provided.

5.  Form your own conclusion from the statistics. If it doesn't match the author's or speaker's, then something is probably wrong.

6.  Determine what information is missing. Be especially alert for misleading numbers and percentages and for missing comparisons.

---

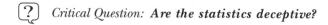 *Critical Question:* **Are the statistics deceptive?**

## Practice Exercises

For each of the practice passages, identify inadequacies in the evidence.

Passage 1

It is time to get those tax-and-spend politicians out of office so that Congress can work to reduce the tax burden on Americans. Today, the typical American family pays 27.3 percent of its income in federal, state, and local taxes. In fact, in 1998, the average household paid over $50,000 in federal income taxes.

Passage 2

"It just isn't safe to drive anymore," my friend lamented, shaking his head as we tooled through Friday afternoon traffic on the freeway. But the fact is, driving in America is safer than it's been in over 60 years. In 1984, we had 18.4 traffic fatalities per 100,000 population, compared to 25.8 in 1970 and 23.3 in 1950. Today you're a lot safer on the road in your car than you are at home or at work. Twelve out of 100 Americans are laid up or need medical attention during the year because of household accidents. Five out of 100 get hurt at work. But only 2.2 per 100 are injured in automobile accidents.

Passage 3

Jennifer: Attorneys are really ripping off the insurance companies. I read that last year attorneys specializing in malpractice cases averaged over $200,000 in the cases that they won.

Anthony: Well, they deserve that money. Doctors are getting more and more careless. In the last three years, the number of patients suing doctors for eye surgery malpractice increased by 25 percent.

Jennifer: Yea, it's scary what's happening to the medical profession. I read somewhere that almost 3 out of 4 people in the country know someone who has sued a doctor; I sure wouldn't want to be a doctor if I had a 75 percent chance of being sued for malpractice.

Anthony: You know, you're right, maybe we should be worried more about losing good doctors because of the high insurance costs. My doctor told me that his insurance rates have increased by 20 percent over the last two years.

Jennifer: You've got a good point. Come to think of it, I saw a petition to ban contingency fees for malpractice cases in the Philadelphia Gazette signed by 200 doctors.

Anthony: You know, Jennifer, I'm think I'm now convinced that the contingency fee for malpractice cases is a mistake; after all, 60 percent of the statistics that we have cited favor that conclusion.

## Sample Responses

Passage 1

CONCLUSION: *A change in Congress is needed so that the tax burden on Americans can be reduced.*

REASON: *The American family pays too much in taxes. The evidence is that the typical American family pays 27.3 percent of its income in federal, state, and local taxes, and the average household paid over $50,000 in federal income taxes.*

Are American families really overtaxed? The words *typical* and *average* should alert us to a potential deception. We need to know what kind of average was used for these statistics. Was it the mean, median, or the mode? For example, if it was the mean, then the values would be greatly inflated by especially affluent households, which pay extremely large amounts of taxes. For example, households making over $1,000,000 dollars, an increasingly common occurrence, would greatly inflate the mean value. The median would give us much lower figures. For example, in 1996, the average household income tax was $48,165, but the median was only $35,536.

There are also important missing comparison figures. For example, how does this tax rate compare to tax rates of previous years? Maybe tax rates have actually decreased.

Passage 2

CONCLUSION: *Driving in America is much safer now than it was 60 years ago.*

REASONS:  1. *Traffic fatalities have decreased greatly from 1950 to 1984.*

2. *It is now safer to drive than it is to stay at home. Data reveal that you are less likely to have an accident in your car than you are at home or at work.*

To evaluate this use of evidence, we should first ask ourselves what would be the most appropriate evidence to address the question, "Is driving in America safer than it used to be?" In our opinion, the best statistic to use to answer that question is a comparison of the rate of serious accidents per specified numbers of miles driven under certain kinds of conditions, for example, city and highway driving between the present and the past. Those are not the figures given in the essay. The figures given are rates per 100,000 population; thus the comparison is deceiving. For example, is the per capita mileage driven in 1984 the same as that driven in 1950 and 1970?

The second set of evidence also represents a deceptive comparison because the figures given fail to take into account the fact that we spend much more time in our offices and in our homes than we do in our cars. The appropriate statistic to be used here would be the rate of accidents per hour spent in each setting; note how that rate differs radically from the percentages actually given. (Note: The argument presented here is similar to arguing that it's safer for a woman to walk in New York's Central Park than to read in her home, because a larger percentage of rapes occur in the home than in parks.)

## CRITICAL QUESTION SUMMARY: WHY THIS QUESTION IS IMPORTANT

### Are the Statistics Deceptive?

Authors often provide statistics to support their reasoning. The statistics appear to be hard evidence. However, there are many ways that statistics can be misused. Because problematic statistics are used frequently, it is important to identify any problems with the statistics so that you can more carefully determine whether you will accept or reject the author's conclusion.

# 12

# WHAT SIGNIFICANT
# INFORMATION IS OMITTED?

How compelling are the following advertisements?

Most doctors prescribe Ease-Pain for headaches!

Coke was Number 1 in recent taste tests!

The purpose of both advertisements is, of course, to persuade you to buy more of the designated product. Even before your critical-thinking skills developed to their current level, you knew that such advertisements tell less than the whole truth. For example, if the Ease-Pain Company gives a bigger discount to hospitals than do other aspirin manufacturers, provides hospitals with greater numbers of free samples, or provides cruises for physicians who use their product, you are unlikely to see this information included in the ad. You will not see that information, but it is quite relevant to your decision about what to take for your headache.

By asking questions learned in previous chapters, such as those concerning ambiguity, assumptions, and evidence, you will detect much important missing information. A more complete search for omitted information, however, is so important to critical evaluation that it deserves further emphasis. This chapter tries to sensitize you even more to the importance of *what is not said* and to serve as an important reminder that we react to an incomplete picture of an argument when we evaluate only the *explicit* parts. We thus devote this chapter to an extremely important additional question you must ask in order to judge the quality of reasoning: What significant information is omitted?

(?)  *Critical Question:* **What significant information is omitted?**

## The Benefits of Detecting Omitted Information

You should remember that almost any information that you encounter has a purpose. In other words, its organization was selected and organized by someone who hoped that it would affect your thinking in some way. Hence, your task is to decide whether you wish to be an instrument of the chosen purpose. Often that purpose is to persuade you.

Advertisers, teachers, politicians, authors, speakers, and parents all organize information to shape your decisions. It is a natural and highly predictable desire on their part. Thus, those trying to persuade you will almost always try to present their position in the strongest possible light. So when you find what you believe to be persuasive reasons—those gold nuggets for which you are prospecting—it's wise to hesitate and to think about what the author may *not* have told you, something that your critical questioning has not yet revealed. Those attractive reasons you found may not be quite so impressive when you realize that their apparent support for the conclusion rests on significant omitted information.

By *significant omitted information,* we mean information that would affect whether you should be influenced by a speaker's or writer's arguments, that is, information that *shapes the reasoning!* Interspersed throughout the chapter will be examples of reasoning that is not very convincing, not because of what is said but because of what is omitted. Study the examples carefully and notice how in each case the failure to look for omitted information would have resulted in your making a premature and potentially erroneous judgment.

## The Certainty of Incomplete Reasoning

Incomplete reasoning is inevitable for several reasons. First, there is the limitation imposed by time and space. Arguments are incomplete because communicators do not have forever to organize them, nor do they have unlimited space or time in which to present their reasons.

Second, most of us have a very limited attention span; we get bored when messages are too long. Thus, communicators often feel a need to get their message across quickly. Advertisements and editorials reflect both these factors. For example, the time or space allotted for presenting an advertising message is short, and the message must both attract and hold our attention. Advertisers consequently engage in many annoying omissions.

A third reason for the inevitability of missing information is that the knowledge possessed by the person making the argument will always be incomplete. A fourth reason why information may be omitted is because of an outright attempt to deceive. Advertisers *know* they are omitting key bits of information. If they were to describe all the chemicals or cheap component parts that go into their products, you would be less likely to buy them. Experts in every field consciously omit information when open disclosure would weaken the persuasive effect of their advice. Such omissions are particularly tempting if those trying to advise you see you as a "sponge."

A final important reason why omitted information is so prevalent is that the values, beliefs, and attitudes of those trying to advise or persuade you are frequently different from yours. You can expect, therefore, that their reasoning will be guided by different assumptions from those you would have brought to the same question. A particular perspective is like a pair of blinders on a horse. The blinders improve the tendency of the horse to focus on what is directly in front of it. Yet, an individual's perspective, like blinders on a horse, prevents that person from noting certain information that would be important to those who reason from a different frame of reference. Unless your perspective is identical to that of the person trying to persuade you, important omissions of information are to be expected.

Let's review. Omitted information is inevitable for at least five reasons.

1.  time and space limitations
2.  limited attention span
3.  inadequacies in human knowledge
4.  deception
5.  existence of different perspectives

## Questions That Identify Omitted Information

If you are now convinced that reasoning will necessarily be incomplete, you may ask, "What am I supposed to do?" Well, initially you have to remind yourself again and again that regardless of how attractive the reasons supporting a particular decision or opinion may be at first glance, it's necessary to take another look in search of omitted information. Remembering to seek missing information is a crucial first step in using this particular critical question.

How do you search, and what can you expect to find? You ask questions to help decide what additional information you need, and then ask questions designed to reveal that information.

Isn't it silly to ask questions of an author who cannot answer? Not at all! Although the writer won't answer your questions, asking her has positive results. First, you may be able to supply the missing information because of what you already know. Second, searching for omitted information in persuasive writing gives you good practice for when you are able to search for omitted information face-to-face with a teacher or anyone else who is trying to persuade you orally. Even more importantly, searching for missing information prevents you from making up your mind too soon. By asking such questions of written material, you are reminding yourself that the information provided is incomplete and that whatever conclusion you reach on the basis of incomplete information will necessarily be very tentative.

There are many different kinds of questions you can use to identify relevant omitted information. Some questions you have already learned to ask will highlight important omitted information. For example, asking critical questions about ambiguity, the use of evidence, and the quality of assumptions usually identifies relevant omitted information.

In addition, to help you determine omitted information that might get overlooked by other critical questions, we provide you below with a list of some important kinds of omitted information and some examples of questions to help detect them.

---

### Clues for Finding Common Kinds of Significant Information

1. **Common counterarguments**
   a.  What reasons would someone who disagrees offer?
   b.  Are there research studies that contradict the studies presented?
   c.  Are there missing examples, testimonials, or analogies that support the other side of the argument?

2. **Missing definitions**
   a.  How would the arguments differ if key terms were defined in other ways?

3. **Missing value preferences or perspectives**
   a. From what other set of values might one approach this issue?
   b. What kinds of arguments would be made by someone approaching the issue from a different set of values?

4. **Origins of "facts" alluded to in the argument**
   a. Where do the "facts" come from?
   b. Are the factual claims supported by competent research or by reliable sources?

5. **Details of procedures used for gathering facts**
   a. How many people completed the questionnaire?
   b. How were the survey questions worded?

6. **Alternative techniques for gathering or organizing the evidence**
   a. How might the results from an interview study differ from written questionnaire results?

7. **Missing or incomplete figures, graphs, tables, or data**
   a. Would the figure look different if it included evidence from earlier or later years?
   b. Has the author "stretched" the figure to make the differences look larger?

8. **Omitted effects, both positive and negative, and both short- and long-term, of what is advocated and what is opposed**
   a. Has the argument left out important positive or negative consequences of a proposed action?
   b. Do we need to know the impact of the action on any of the following areas: political, social, economic, biological, spiritual, health, or environmental?

9. **Context of quotes and testimonials**
   a. Has a quote or testimonial been taken out of context?

10. **Benefits accruing to the author from convincing others to follow her advice**
   a. Will the author benefit financially if we adopt her proposed policy?

Being aware of these specific types should help you a lot in locating relevant omitted information. Because there are so many kinds of important omitted information, however, you should always ask yourself the general question,

"Has the speaker or writer left out any other information that I need to know before I judge the quality of her reasoning?"

Let's examine some arguments that have omitted some of the types of information just listed and watch how each omission might cause us to form a faulty conclusion. Only by asking that omitted information be supplied in each case could you avoid this danger. Initially, let's look at an advertising claim.

A well-known mouthwash commercial boasts that the mouthwash has new powerful ingredients that kill 90 percent of the bacteria that cause bad breath. Should we thus conclude that we should buy this advertised brand of mouthwash? Wait just a minute! Among many omissions, the advertisement neglects to include any information about: (a) what percentage of bacteria other mouthwashes kill; maybe they kill 95 percent of the bacteria; (b) amount of bacteria killed by regular brushing of teeth or by simply swishing water around in our mouth; maybe our breath is fine as long as we brush our teeth; (c) potential negative consequences of killing mouth bacteria; maybe a certain amount of bacteria is necessary for a healthy mouth; (d) other causes of bad breath; maybe tonsils and sinus infections contribute; (e) how much bacteria are needed to cause bad breath; maybe 10 percent is enough; (f) the effect of the mouthwash on the inside of the mouth; might it harm our gums? (g) other advantages and disadvantages of the mouthwash, such as taste, price, and length of effective action. The advertiser has omitted much significant data that you would need if you were to buy wisely.

Do you see how advertising phrases like "doctor recommended," "it's the real thing," "reduced calories," "light," "98 percent fat free," "fiber rich," "can help to reduce cholesterol," and "100 percent natural," may all be accurate but misleading because of omitted information?

It's pretty obvious that advertising omits much relevant information. Let's now take a look at a more complicated reasoning example. Read the following excerpt and ask yourself what has been omitted, referring to our list for clues to your search.

Women in our society are paying a steep price for feminism's push for increased equality. By delaying marriage to pursue careers, women encounter a severe "man shortage," endangering their opportunity for marriage. For example, a recent marriage study by Harvard and Yale researchers found that a college-educated, unwed woman at 30 has a 20 percent likelihood of marriage, and at 35, a 5 percent chance. In addition, there has been a major plunge in economic status afflicting women who divorce under the new no-fault law. A study by a sociologist found that the average woman suffers a 73 percent drop in her living standard a year after divorce, while the average man enjoys a 40 percent rise. Also, women's mental health has never been worse and is declining in direct proportion to women's tendency to stay single or devote themselves to careers. In fact, single women now make up the great majority of psychotherapists' practice.

What important information do you need to know before you can decide whether feminists should stop pushing for equality with men? Let us suggest some questions.

What common counterarguments or counterexamples might feminists use to refute this reasoning? We can imagine counterarguments that stress the positive consequences of seeking greater equality, such as increased diversity in job choices and domestic roles, increased legal rights, and increased reproductive freedom.

What are possible definitions of mental health that might be used in this argument? What value assumptions do these definitions reflect?

What is the origin of the facts alluded to in the argument? How does the author know that women's mental health has declined and that single women dominate psychotherapists' offices and that the average woman suffers a 73 percent drop in her living standard? Also, how confident can we be of the calculation of marital odds? The research appears to originate from university settings, but the author presents too little detail for us to judge the quality of the research.

For example, is it helpful to you to know that in a more recent study than the one cited, another university researcher sampled 13.4 million households, instead of the 60,000 sampled in the cited study, and found that at 30, never-married, college-educated women have a 58 to 66 percent chance at marriage, and at 35 the odds were 32 to 41 percent, seven times higher than the Harvard-Yale figure? We would surely want to know the basis for this difference before we judge the quality of the evidence cited.

Would other research methods give us a different view of women's happiness? For example, we can tell you that a study in the 90s, which tracked the same women for more than three decades, reported that "traditional" married women ran a higher risk of developing mental and physical ailments in their lifetime than single women—from depression to migraines, from high blood pressure to colitis. Also, a Louis Harris poll of women between the ages of 45 and 60 reported that the majority of them said they didn't want to get married.

How do the living standards of divorced women and men differ after *five* years? Obviously, the author gave you only a partial picture of how feminist goals of equality have affected women. Unless you complete the picture, your decision about whether to support feminist goals will be very uninformed.

## The Importance of the Negative View

There is one type of omitted information that we believe is so important to identify and so often overlooked that we want to specifically highlight it for you: the *potential negative effects* of actions being advocated, such as new technology, industrial expansion, and public policy. We stress the negative effects here because usually proposals for such action come into existence in the context of backers' heralding their benefits, such as greater choice and speed, better appearance, more leisure, increased length of life, and more and/or improved commodities. However, because most actions have such widespread positive *and negative* impacts, we need to ask:

---

- Which segments of society do *not* benefit from a proposed action? Who loses? What do the losers have to say about it?

- How does the proposed action affect the distribution of power?

- Does the action influence the extent of democracy in our society?

- How does a particular action affect how we view the world: what we think, how we think, and what we know and can know?

- What are the action's effects on our health?

- How does the action influence our relationships with one another? With the natural environment?

- Will the action have a slow, cumulative impact?

---

For each of these questions, we always also want to ask, "What are the potential *long-term negative effects* of the action?"

To illustrate the usefulness of asking these omitted-information questions, let's reflect upon the following question: What are some possible negative effects of increasing advances in computer technology, a policy advocated by many in our society? Did you think of the following?

- *Pollution and impaired health.* For example, does computer manufacturing use large amounts of toxic materials that must eventually be disposed of at toxic dumps? Also, what is the effect on our health of lengthy periods in front of a computer terminal?

- *Shifts in employment.* How many people might lose their jobs or have to shift to less interesting jobs?

- *Invasion of privacy.* How easy will it be for others to possess information about our incomes and our personal habits?

- *Information acceleration.* What is the effect on human beings of an information overload?

- *Military centralization.* Is it possible that with increased connections among supercomputers, individual groups in our society might gain too much power over military actions?

- *Decreases in social interactions.* How much time will be absorbed by interacting with machines, rather than people?

Questions such as these can give us pause for thought before jumping on the bandwagon of a proposed action.

## Omitted Information That Remains Missing

Just because you are able to request important missing information, does not guarantee a satisfactory response. It is quite possible that your probing questions cannot be answered. Do not despair! You did your part. You requested information that you needed to make up your mind; you must now decide whether it is possible to arrive at a conclusion without the missing information. We warned you earlier that reasoning is always incomplete. Therefore, to claim automatically that you cannot make a decision as long as information is missing would prevent you from ever forming any opinions.

## USING THIS CRITICAL QUESTION

Once you have thought about the existence of missing information in an argument, what should you do? The first logical reaction is to seek the information. But usually you will encounter resistance. Your options as a critical thinker are to voice your displeasure with the argument in light of the missing information, keep searching for the information that you require, or cautiously agree with the reasoning on the grounds that this argument is better than its competitors.

## Missing Information and Your Own Writing and Speaking

When you communicate, you will necessarily omit some information that your audience needs. However, at the same time, your experience using this critical question as an evaluative tool should forewarn you that some information is especially important for a strong argument. When you write or speak, you show respect for your audience when you include specific information that you know in advance will assist them in deciding the merits of your reasoning.

For example, when you propose an action, think about the disadvantages of what you are advocating and share those problems with your audience. To do otherwise is to insult them. They know there are disadvantages, so in the interest of your own integrity, be open about their existence.

 *Critical Question:* **What significant information is omitted?**

## Practice Exercises

In each of the following examples, there is important missing information. Make a list of questions you would ask the person who wrote each passage. Explain in each case why the information you are seeking is important to you as you try to decide the worth of the reasoning.

Passage 1

Students need more sleep. Their performance on papers and exams deteriorates as they get less sleep. Again and again, when honors students are asked about their sleep habits, they tell us that they get a lot of sleep.

Further, we have all seen the late-night parade of students coming home late from the bars. Our counseling center published a pamphlet that documented the fact that these late-night carousers are often the very students who are eventually dismissed from campus because of poor grades. A little more sleep might have rescued them.

Passage 2

Researchers long have sought a "morning-after" pill that could make birth control safer and more effective than it is today. A study in Scotland suggests that such a pill may soon be available. But abortion opponents are trying to block its use in the United States. The study tested small doses of RU-486, the controversial French abortion drug on 402 women, and no pregnancies resulted. The drug caused fewer side effects than the less-than-satisfactory morning-after pills available from doctors today. If tested and eventually sold here, RU-486 might save women from undergoing abortions and from running gauntlets of screaming, sign-waving protestors. RU-486 is relatively safe, simple, and cheap. We need to stop the abortion opponents from blocking the use of RU-486 in the United States.

Passage 3

Every day, we read about another state that wants to legalize gambling and open casinos. Puritanical politicians denounce such laws. But a look at the data suggests that these politicians are greatly overreacting. Gambling is not the poison to our society that so many people think it is.

Many are concerned about people becoming addicted to gambling. But a recent study by researchers at Harvard Medical School's Division on Addictions provides evidence to refute this belief. It found that about 1.6 percent of American adults will become pathological gamblers, compared with 6.2 percent who will succumb to drug addiction and 13.8 percent who will become alcoholics. Another concern raised by many is that gambling addiction is increasing suicide rates, but again evidence suggests this is not the case. Although Nevada has a high suicide rate, other states that are the home of many casinos, for example, Mississippi and New Jersey, have suicide rates that fall below the national average.

As for the argument that legal gambling fosters crime, no consistent relationship has been found between the existence of casinos and the prevalence of crime. The lack of such a relationship is supported by the experience of the states of Illinois and Colorado, in which many new casinos have been recently introduced. In both states, academic and police experts have testified that they have not noticed an increase in criminal activity.

Another argument often used against gambling is that it causes corruption; it's too much money in the wrong hands. There is much concern that casino operators are exerting too much influence on our politicians. But if you look at the "soft money" given to politicians from the two major political parties during the last election year, the gambling industry ranked only 16th in the number of contributions to politicians.

## Sample Responses

Passage 1

CONCLUSION: *College students would do better in school if they would get more sleep.*

REASONS:   1. *High achieving students claim that they sleep a lot.*
   2. *The counseling center at our school says that students who stay out late at night are often the same students required to leave school because of poor grades.*

Before we all start insisting on more sleep, we should pause to take another look at the information provided to lead to this conclusion. What are the counterarguments, for example? Is it possible that staying up late frequently to do your work especially well might lead to better grades? And, just how much more sleep do honors students get? Would they do even better in school if they slept a little less?

Further, just what do we know about how the honors students were surveyed? Nothing at all! Finally, does the counseling center have any persuasive evidence that those who stay out late indeed are the same group of students who have the lowest grades?

These are just a few of the questions we would want to ask before we relied on the information in this passage.

Passage 2

CONCLUSION: *The United States needs to pursue the possible use of RU-486, the French abortion drug.*

REASONS:   1. *A study in Scotland shows it is safe and causes fewer side effects than other available drugs.*
2. *The drug can save women from undergoing abortions and from confronting radical protestors.*

First, we should note that this reasoning advocates pursuing a new technology—a morning-after pill—and cites only its advantages. The writer omits possible disadvantages. We need to consider both advantages and disadvantages. What serious side effects might come from frequent, long-term use of the drug? What positive and negative effects might such a drug have on how men and women relate to each other sexually? Might people become less reflective about their sexual behavior? Would its availability make it easier for men to exploit women? Could its presence lead to less emphasis on "safe sex" and thus cause more AIDS cases? The advantages of the drug may well outweigh the disadvantages, but we need to be aware of both in judging the merits of the conclusion.

Furthermore, much relevant information is missing about the research. How were these women selected? Are they typical in terms of physical health? How many side effects are indicated by the phrase "fewer side effects"? How severe are the side effects? What do other research studies of this drug show? Getting answers to a number of questions would help us decide whether we want to fight efforts to block RU-486.

CRITICAL QUESTION SUMMARY:
WHY THIS QUESTION IS IMPORTANT

### What Significant Information Is Omitted?

When an author is trying to persuade you of something, he or she often leaves out important information. This information is often useful in assessing the worth of that information. By explicitly looking for omitted information, you can determine whether the author has provided you with enough information to support the reasoning. If she has left out too much information, you cannot accept the information as support for the conclusion. Consequently, you should choose to reject her conclusion.

# 13

# WHAT REASONABLE CONCLUSIONS ARE POSSIBLE?

By this stage you should be better equipped to pan for intellectual gold—to distinguish stronger reasons from weaker ones. In descriptive arguments, strong reasons will be persuasive relevant evidence such as findings of a careful research study, a relevant analogy, an appeal to a reliable authority, or compelling examples. For prescriptive arguments, the strong reasons will be principles or descriptive statements you identify as best supported and most relevant.

Consider the following argument:

> It is time to end the divorce revolution we have been experiencing over the past 30 years. It has created economic insecurity for many mothers and caused untold numbers of fathers to walk away from financial responsibility for their children. In addition, countless children are experiencing the negative impacts of divorce. Thus, repealing no-fault divorce laws in cases involving children makes a lot of sense. By making divorces more difficult to obtain, more parents will stay together and work out their difficulties, reducing the divorce rate.

Should you urge your local congressman to support the repeal of no-fault divorce laws? Suppose that you checked the author's reasons and found them believable. Are there other conclusions that might be equally consistent with these reasons as the author's conclusion? The chapter summary will suggest several alternative conclusions that are possible.

Very rarely will you have a situation in which only one conclusion can be reasonably inferred. Consequently, you must make sure that the conclusion you eventually adopt is the most reasonable and the most consistent with your value preferences. The recognition that the reasons could provide support for conclusions different from yours should heighten your interest in any further tests or studies that would help identify the best conclusion.

[?]  *Critical Question:* **What reasonable conclusions are possible?**

## Assumptions and Multiple Conclusions

Neither evidence attempting to support a factual claim nor a group of strong reasons supporting a prescriptive conclusion can be interpreted in only one way. Reasons do not generally speak for themselves in an obvious way. As we have seen many times, conclusions are reached only after someone makes certain interpretations or assumptions concerning the meaning of the reasons.

If you make a different assumption concerning the meaning of the reasons, you will reach different conclusions. Because we all possess different levels of perceptual precision, frames of reference, and prior knowledge, we repeatedly disagree about which conclusions are preferable. We form different conclusions from reasons because our diverse backgrounds and goals cause us to be attracted to different assumptions when we decide to link reasons to conclusions.

Sometimes a writer or speaker will mention alternative conclusions that can be reached on the basis of the reasons he has presented. However, you will often have to generate possible alternatives. To perform this creative task, try to imagine what different assumptions might enable someone to jump from the reasons you have identified to another conclusion. Remember, *many* possible conclusions can be made on the basis of most sets of reasons. The next two sections help you recognize the multiplicity of possible conclusions.

## Dichotomous Thinking: Impediment to Considering Multiple Conclusions

Very few important questions can be answered with a simple "yes" or an absolute "no." When people think in black or white, yes or no, right or wrong, or correct or incorrect terms, they engage in *dichotomous thinking*. This type of thinking consists of assuming there are only two possible answers to a question that has multiple potential answers.

We encountered dichotomous thinking earlier when we discussed the Either-Or fallacy. This fallacy, and dichotomous thinking in general, damages reasoning by overly restricting our vision. We think we are finished after considering two optional decisions, thereby overlooking many options and the positive consequences that could have resulted from choosing one of them.

Dichotomous thinkers often are rigid and intolerant because they fail to understand the importance of context for a particular answer. To see this point more clearly, imagine this situation:

Your roommate asks you to help plan her ethics paper. The paper is to address the question: Should a person tell the truth? In her mind, the paper requires her to defend a "yes" or "no" position.

You have learned that dichotomous thinking can be avoided by qualifying conclusions, by putting them into context. This qualification process requires you to ask about any conclusion:

1.  *When* is it accurate?

2.  *Where* is it accurate?

3.  *Why* or *for what purpose* is it accurate?

You then begin to apply this process to the paper assignment.

Would you be surprised by your roommate's growing frustration as you explained that at certain specified times, in certain situations, to maximize particular values or objectives one should tell the truth? She's looking for "yes" or "no"; you provided a complicated "it depends on . . ."

Rigid, dichotomous thinking limits the range of your decisions and opinions. Even worse, it overly simplifies complex situations. As a consequence, dichotomous thinkers are high-risk candidates for confusion.

The next section illustrates the restrictive effects of dichotomous thinking.

## Two Sides or Many?

Before we look at several arguments in which multiple conclusions are possible, let's make sure you appreciate the large number of conclusions that are possible with respect to most important controversies. Here are three contemporary questions.

1.  Do IQ tests measure intelligence?

2.  Is the president's tax proposal desirable?

3.  Should judges be elected or appointed?

At first glance, these questions and many like them seem to call for yes or no answers. However, a qualified yes or no is often the best answer. The advantage of *maybe* as an answer is that it forces you to admit that you do not yet know enough to make a definite answer. But at the same time you avoid a definite answer, you form a tentative decision or opinion that calls for commitment and eventual action. Once you recognize that you can never be certain how to answer a complex question, you can better accept the necessity of making decisions even when you know you are missing critical information or understanding. It's wise to seek additional information that would improve the support for your opinions, but at some point you must stop searching and make a decision, even when the most forceful answer you are willing to defend is a "yes, but . . ."

Glance back at the three questions that preceded the last paragraph. Ask yourself what conclusions would be possible in response to each question. Naturally, a simple yes or a no answer would be two possible conclusions. Are there others? Yes, there are many! Let's look at just a few of the possible answers to the first of these questions.

---

### Do IQ Tests Measure Intelligence?

1. Yes, to the extent that intelligence means sequential reasoning.

2. Yes, when they are given to children with the same sociocultural background.

3. Yes, if they are used for only elementary children.

4. Yes, when the IQ scores are highly correlated with measures of motivation.

5. Yes, but only in terms of the type of intelligence that is useful in schools.

6. No, if you define intelligence as that factor which leads to later success in one's chosen field.

7. No, if they failed to include data gathered orally.

---

Notice that in each case we added a condition that is necessary before their conclusion can be justified. In the absence of any data or definitions, any of these seven conclusions could be most reasonable. These seven are just a few of the conclusions possible for the first question. Thus, there may be many possible answers to a question, not just two.

Just for practice, try to suggest five possible conclusions for the third question: Should judges be elected or appointed?

Perhaps this conclusion occurred to you: *Elected, if it can be demonstrated that most of those who would vote understand the tasks of a judge well enough to make a choice consistent with efficient justice.* Or, maybe you thought of this one: *Appointed, in those states where the voter turnout in state legislative races has averaged less than 50 percent in the last ten years.* But probably neither of these appears on your list. Why are we so sure? Because there are an enormous number of possible conclusions for this question. It should be an unlikely coincidence if you had chosen either of these two from the huge list of possible conclusions. This greater number of answers is what we want you to grasp. Knowledge of the possibility of multiple conclusions will prevent you from leaping to one prematurely.

## Searching for Multiple Conclusions

This section contains two arguments that point out multiple conclusions that could be created from the reasons in each argument. The intention is to give you some models to use when you search for conclusions. In each case, we will give you the structure of the argument before we suggest alternative conclusions. One clue to help you in your search is the following: Study the reasons without looking at the conclusion, and try to identify as many conclusions as possible that would follow from the reasons. You can always use the when, where, and why questions to help generate alternative conclusions.

> CONCLUSION: *There should be no law restricting access to alcohol.*
>
> REASONS:  1. *Any young person who wants alcohol badly enough can get it, regardless of his or her age.*
>  2. *Many countries permit even little children to have a glass of wine with their meals, and these countries have not been negatively affected.*

Let's start by accepting these reasons as sensible to us. What do we then make of them? We have one answer in the conclusion of the writer: abandon all legislative restrictions on access to alcohol.

But even when we accept these two reasons, we would not necessarily conclude the same thing. Other conclusions make at least as much sense on the basis of this support. For example, it would follow that we should restrict access to alcohol, except in the young person's own home where the parents could guide consumption habits.

Or, alternatively, these reasons might suggest that we need much stricter alcohol statutes to prevent what is claimed in the first reason. Then, out of respect for the second reason, we would add to these new strict statutes a provision excluding wine consumption in the home. Not only are these two alternative conclusions logically supported by the reasons, they lead to conclusions that are quite different from the original conclusion.

CONCLUSION:   *Congress should not decriminalize marijuana.*

REASONS:   1. *A group of British scientists has shown that smoking marijuana may cause serious brain damage.*
2. *Marijuana smokers risk decreasing their fertility.*
3. *Marijuana smokers often become heroin users.*

What conclusions are possible? One would be to decriminalize marijuana in one locale and observe the impact before making a national rule. Alternatively, Congress could sponsor research designed to develop a substance that would produce effects similar to those produced by marijuana without the possible side effects. Another possibility, based on a strong devotion to the value of individual responsibility, would be to permit pot to be sold in stores along with other possibly hazardous materials, the assumption being that those who may misuse the drug have a right to do so. Observe that all three of these conclusions are possible even if we accept the truth of the three reasons. Thus, the same reasons frequently can be used to support several different conclusions.

## Productivity of If-Clauses

If you went back over all the alternative conclusions discussed in this chapter, you would notice that each optional conclusion is possible because we are missing certain information, definitions, assumptions, or the frame of reference of the person analyzing the reasons. Consequently, we can create multiple conclusions by the judicious use of *if-clauses*. In an if-clause, we state a condition that we are assuming in order to enable us to reach a particular conclusion. Notice that the use of if-clauses permits us to arrive at a conclusion without pretending that we know more than we actually do about a particular controversy.

When you use if-clauses to precede conclusions, you are pointing out that your conclusion is based on particular claims or assumptions about which you are uncertain. To see what we mean, look at the following sample conditional statements that might precede conclusions.

1.  If freedom of religion is meant when the writer speaks of the loss of our basic freedom, then . . .

2.  If the birthrate continues to rise over the next five years, then . . .

3.  If it can be proven that most of those using the insanity defense today are truly mentally ill, then . . .

If-clauses present you with multiple conclusions that you may wish to assess before making up your mind about the controversy, and they also broaden the list of possible conclusions from which you can choose your opinion.

## Alternative Solutions as Conclusions

We frequently encounter issues posed in the following form:

> Should we do X?
>
> Is X desirable?

Such questions naturally "pull" for dichotomous thinking. Often, however, posing questions in this manner hides a broader question, "What should we do about Y?" (usually some pressing problem). Rewording the question in this way leads us to generate multiple conclusions of a particular form: solutions to the problems raised by the reasons. Generating multiple solutions greatly increases the flexibility of our thinking.

Let's examine the following passage to illustrate the importance of generating multiple solutions as possible conclusions.

> Should we outlaw those nudist beaches on the edge of our community? We certainly should. Look at the traffic problems they are causing and the hundreds of cars that have been parking illegally since the beach opened.

Once we change this question to, "What should we do about the traffic and parking problems?" a number of possible solutions come to mind, which help us formulate our conclusion to the issue. For example, we might conclude: "No, we should not outlaw the nudist beaches; we should have police vigorously enforce the no-parking rules and have the park service restrict the number of people allowed on the beach."

When reasons in a prescriptive argument are statements of practical problems, look for different solutions to the problems as possible conclusions.

---

### Clues for Identifying Alternative Conclusions

1. Try to identify as many conclusions as possible that would follow from the reasons.

2. Use *if-clauses* to qualify alternative conclusions.

3. Reword the issue to "What should we do about Y?"

---

## The Liberating Effect of Recognizing Alternative Conclusions

If logic, facts, or studies were self-explanatory, we would approach learning in a particular manner. Our task would be to have someone else, a teacher perhaps, provide the beliefs that we should have. Specifically, we would seek that single identifiable set of beliefs that logic and facts dictate.

While we have tremendous respect for logic and facts, we cannot exaggerate their worth as guides for conclusion formation. They take us only so far; then we have to go the rest of the way toward belief, using the help that facts and logic have provided.

A first step in using that help is the search for possible multiple conclusions consistent with logic and the facts as we know them. This search liberates us in an important way. It frees us from the inflexible mode of learning sketched above. Once we recognize the variety of possible conclusions, each of us can experience the excitement of enhanced personal choice.

We want to warn you that the rewarding feeling that often comes with generating multiple conclusions may tempt you to treat them as equally credible and to believe your job is done after you've made your list. But remember that some conclusions can be better justified than others, and the most believable ones should be the ones that most affect your reaction to the author's reasoning. Thus, after you have applied your creative-thinking skills to make your list of multiple conclusions, you will then want to carefully consider the credibility of each.

## Summary

Very rarely do reasons mean just one thing. After evaluating a set of reasons, you still must decide what conclusion is most consistent with the best reasons in the controversy. To avoid dichotomous thinking in your search for the strongest conclusion, provide alternative contexts for the conclusions through the use of when, where, and why questions.

Qualifications for conclusions will move you away from dichotomous thinking. If-clauses provide a technique for expressing these qualifications.

For instance, let's take another look at the argument for repealing no-fault divorce laws at the beginning of the chapter. What alternative conclusions might be consistent with the reasons given?

AUTHOR'S CONCLUSION:  *No-fault divorce laws need to be repealed.*

ALTERNATIVE CONCLUSIONS:  1. *If freedom of choice is more important than financial security, then we should not repeal no-fault divorce laws.*

2. *If it can be shown that repealing no-fault laws creates additional family conflicts by pitting parents against each other and forcing children to choose sides, then a better solution to the author's concerns might be to work toward reducing such conflicts, perhaps by encouraging greater use of divorce mediation instead of litigation.*

3. *If it can be demonstrated that no-fault divorce laws are not a major cause of increased divorce rates, or a much less important cause than such factors as increases in dual-career marriages or changes in parental roles, then the no-fault laws should not be changed.*

Many more alternative conclusions are possible in light of the author's reasons. Considering them would improve the quality of our response.

## Practice Exercises

⟨?⟩  *Critical Question:* **What reasonable conclusions are possible?**

For each of the following arguments, identify different conclusions that could be drawn from the reasons.

### Passage 1

When people are required to live together, there are bound to be numerous problems. Students all over our campus are moving out of their dormitory rooms because they have been uncomfortable in their previous living arrangements. The solution to this problem is to prevent the problems before they begin.

If the Housing Office would make it a practice to send out personality surveys and interest inventories before students ever set foot on campus, they could pair roommates who have something in common. The Housing Office is letting us all down when it permits the discomfort associated with trying to live with an incompatible roommate.

Passage 2

When I bought a computer three months ago and began using it for educational purposes, my grades went up by an average of half a letter grade. *Consumer Reports* also said that some computers have been specially designed for educational purposes, a clear indication that they will improve school performance. Therefore, each student, upon entering college, should be required to buy a computer.

Passage 3

As you are driving on our increasingly crowded highways, you see more and more and bigger and bigger SUVs passing by. Criticism of SUVs has increased over the last few years, and their reputation has gotten so bad that even late night comedians are making fun of them on a regular basis. Is the mounting derision of SUVs justified? I believe it is more than justified. The case against SUVs is not just a matter of taste. SUVs are directly harming the public in a number of ways.

The biggest problem is that they are killing many Americans. Driving an SUV more than doubles the chance that you will kill someone else in a crash, according to a recent national study. This is because they weigh much more than regular cars and their chassis are higher. When they hit another car, they crush it. Evidence that they are more dangerous than regular cars is provided by a recent study in which it was found that SUVs colliding with cars killed more people than cars colliding with cars.

And despite the beliefs of many that they are safer inside SUVs because they are so big and heavy, fatality rates for people inside SUVs are about the same as for those inside regular cars. You and your family are just as likely to die when riding in a large SUV as you are when riding in a midsize car, according to a study by the National Automobile Safety Council. Why is this? Because SUVs increase the likelihood that you will die in a rollover. For example, if you roll over in an SUV, you're 10 times more likely to be killed than if you roll over in a Honda Civic.

Also, SUVs are polluting our environment because they are exempt from rules that apply to standard cars. Present law permits them to emit more than 5 times as much pollution per mile. Imagine what the smog in our cities will look like if we continue the SUV buying mania.

It's time for Americans to wake up and stop buying SUVs, unless they have some real need for such a huge, unsafe, polluting vehicle.

## Sample Responses

### Passage 1

CONCLUSION: *The Housing Office is failing in its responsibilities to the students.*

REASONS:   1. *Large numbers of roommates have problems.*
            2. *Discomfort among roommates is preventable.*
            3. *Matching students' interests would make them more comfortable.*

To work on this particular critical-thinking skill, we need to assume that the reasons are strong ones. If we accept these reasons as reliable, we could also reasonably infer the following conclusions:

*If the Housing Office's major goal is encouraging interaction among diverse students, one conclusion might be that they are doing their job effectively.*

*The legally responsible Housing Office should petition the legislature to permit an exception to the current laws requiring it to match students according to the diversity guidelines handed down by the Attorney General's Office.*

Notice that both alternative conclusions put the Housing Office in quite a different light compared to the negative portrayal it received in the original conclusion.

### Passage 2

CONCLUSION: *Each college student should be required to buy a computer.*

REASON:   1. *When the author bought a computer three months ago, his grades increased by an average of half a letter grade*
            2. *Some computers are made solely for educational purposes.*

On the basis of these reasons, we could infer several alternative conclusions:

*Students who are similar to the author should use computers for educational purposes.*

*If individual responsibility is preferable to collective responsibility, and a student wishes to improve her grades, she should buy a computer for educational purposes.*

*If it can be demonstrated that students will not effectively use computers supplied in central locations, then colleges should provide computers in each dorm room.*

## CRITICAL QUESTION SUMMARY: WHY THIS QUESTION IS IMPORTANT

### What Reasonable Conclusions Are Possible?

When you are deciding whether to accept or reject an author's conclusion, you want to make sure that the author has come to the most reasonable conclusion. An author often oversteps his or her reasoning when he or she comes to a conclusion. By identifying alternative reasonable conclusions, you can determine which alternative conclusions, if any, you would be willing to accept in place of the author's conclusion. This step is the final tool in deciding whether to accept or reject the author's conclusion.

# 14

# PRACTICE AND REVIEW

In this chapter, we put it all together for you. We will begin by again listing the critical questions. This checklist should serve as a handy guide for you until the questions become second nature. When you encounter articles, lectures, debates, textbooks, commercials, Internet messages, or any other materials relating to an issue that is important to you, you will find it useful to go through the checklist and check off each question as you ask it.

Next we apply the critical questions by critically evaluating one position on a contemporary controversy. The major purpose of this discussion is to provide an example of a coherent application of all the critical-thinking steps.

We suggest that you follow the discussion with several goals in mind. You can treat it as a check on your understanding of previous chapters. Would you have asked the same questions? Would you have formed similar answers? Do you feel better able to judge the worth of someone's reasoning?

## Question Checklist for Critical Thinking

1.   What are the issue and the conclusion?
2.   What are the reasons?
3.   What words or phrases are ambiguous?
4.   What are the value conflicts and assumptions?
5.   What are the descriptive assumptions?
6.   Are there any fallacies in the reasoning?

7. How good is the evidence?

8. Are there rival causes?

9. Are the statistics deceptive?

10. What significant information is omitted?

11. What reasonable conclusions are possible?

## Asking the Right Questions: A Comprehensive Example

We first present a passage that summarizes one position with respect to whether parental consent should be required for a minor to obtain an abortion. This section is followed by a lengthy discussion based on all 11 critical-thinking questions.

Teenagers face extremely complicated social and emotional issues. The issues are inescapable, but most teens are not prepared to rationally handle them. Because they are ill prepared, the need for effective and honest communication between teens and their parents is more vital than ever. Parents' wisdom, accumulated by their experience and study, can guide their children to the best decision. This pressing need for communication is being undermined however, by the extension of individual rights to minors.

A troubling example of a minor's rights taken much too far is the federal law that permits minors to obtain an abortion without parental consent. The reasoning behind such a law is that a girl will be less likely to get the abortion she wants if she must disclose her intentions to her parents. What these supporters fail to consider is that just because a minor *wants* to get an abortion does not mean she *should* get one. Think about it. Would you want your daughter to make an impulsive decision about such an important matter? This law needs to be changed before more teenagers' lives are destroyed.

Compare the situation with that of a young child who is terribly distraught over a particular bully's constant taunting. The child may want to retort with nasty remarks or a physical fight. Only after consulting with a parent will the child realize that a confrontation yields more aggravation and possible physical harm.

Similarly, a girl who discovers she is pregnant will be overcome with emotions—regret, confusion, guilt, disappointment, and fear. With these emotions weighing upon her, she is likely to act unthinkingly. She needs the mature and rational guidance a parent can provide to avoid making an impulsive decision.

Supporters also argue that involuntary parental consent will only damage the parent/child relationship by escalating conflict and stress. Just the opposite is the case, however. Parental consent requirements prevent disastrous scenes that will inevitably occur if parents discover their daughter has had an abortion without their consent.

Of course, some tensions may arise when the daughter reveals her pregnancy, but this initial tension is a small price to pay for an open and honest relationship. Statutes that allow abortions to be administered without parental consent prevent girls from seeking the advice of the people who care so much for them.

These anti-parental-consent laws developed out of a legitimate concern for a minor's rights, but what about the rights of the parents? Law requires parental consent when a minor is to undergo any medical procedure. A minor can be refused medical attention until one parent consents, except in emergency situations. This law even applies to a minor's wish to get her ears pierced! In such cases, the law recognizes the parents' right to know the state of their child's well being. It is a denial of this right, therefore, to permit minors to undergo the medical procedure of an abortion without parental consent. If the government considers the safety and health of a minor so important, then it should protect that safety in all instances.

Also, parents need to know if their child has had an abortion in case she suffers any physical or emotional side effects, which are nearly inevitable. In a survey of gynecologists, 91 percent had treated patients with complications from legal abortions. These complications included uncontrollable bleeding, hemorrhaging, seizures, infections, abdominal pains, and cervical lacerations.

Equally damaging are the psychological effects, such as Post-Traumatic Stress Disorder and depression. A recent research study shows that teenage girls who have experienced abortion tend to experience depression at a much higher rate than do those who have not. Perhaps most frightening is another study showing that 60 percent of women who have post-abortion trauma have suicidal thoughts.

If parents are unaware that their daughter has undergone an abortion, then how can they be attentive to the warning signs for suicide and the other disorders? The answer is that they can't; and without proper treatment, these side effects may become more damaging to the girl's health than if they were attended to immediately.

Those who disagree with parental consent requirements often cite well-known organizations that share their view, such as Planned Parenthood. But Planned Parenthood rejects the requirements for economic reasons rather than ideological ones. The organization's caseload of teen pregnancies decreases by as much as 85 percent in states where parental consent is mandatory for an abortion by a minor. The result of a reduced caseload is a reduced cash flow. Obviously, Planned Parenthood is not going to support a practice that is not profitable for them.

Not everyone is deceived by these organizations' professed support. In several polls, over 70 percent of people surveyed were in favor of parental notification laws. Also, many religious organizations have voiced strong support for such laws. Yet, liberal courts and an unresponsive government are failing to address the public's wishes. What the courts and the government do not understand is the importance of fostering communication between children and parents on the sensitive issues of the day.

## What Are the Issue and the Conclusion?

The issue addressed in the previous passage is a prescriptive one: Should parental consent be required for a minor to obtain an abortion? We know that this is the issue because of what the writer seeks to prove. The author's reasons all support the conclusion that yes, parental consent should be required. The reasons emphasize problems with the present law and advantages of repealing it. Also, sentence 11 explicitly signals the conclusion by its use of the indicator words "needs to be."

## What Are the Reasons?

Let's paraphrase the reasons that lead to the conclusion that parental consent should be required in order for a minor to have an abortion.

1.  The need for effective communication is more vital than ever, and this law undermines such communications.

    Supporting reason: Most teens can't handle complicated social and emotional issues by themselves.

2.  Minors are too emotional and impulsive to make such decisions; just because they want an abortion does not mean they should get one.

    Supporting reason: The abortion decision is like reacting to a bully; emotions outweigh rationality.

3.  Consent laws will not escalate conflict and stress; just the opposite will be true.

4.  Such a law denies the parental rights that are granted when minors undergo medical procedures.

5.  Parental knowledge of an abortion will reduce the impact of inevitable physical and emotional side effects.

Supporting reason: Ninety-one percent of gynecologists have treated patients with complications, such as uncontrolled bleeding, hemorrhaging, and so on.

Supporting reason two: Research shows an association between having an abortion and experiencing depression.

6.  We should not attend to Planned Parenthood arguments because it has an economic investment in maintaining the law.

7.  The American people favor parental notification laws.

Supporting reason: A survey shows that 70 percent of people favor them.

8.  Religious organizations favor notification laws.


## What Words or Phrases Are Ambiguous?

We look first for possible ambiguity that might weaken the reasoning presented by focusing on the author's major reasons. An important ambiguity pervades the entire argument. What precisely is meant by "parental consent"?

The phrase may appear clear—a parent must say it is permissible for the minor to have the abortion—but it could be interpreted several different ways. In fact, the interpretations of "parental consent" vary from state to state. Notice how your reaction to parental consent notification laws would be affected by the choice of either of the following alternative definitions of parental consent.

   A. *Permission from either parent.*

   B. *Permission from both parents, except in a divorce situation, in which consent must be obtained from the parent who has custody.*

   C. *Permission from both parents, with no exceptions.*

If you believe, for example, that requiring the consent from both parents creates too much family stress, you may be less supportive of the conclusion if the writer means the third definition.

In addition, the passage does not specify who can legally be considered a parent. Grandparents today are raising many children. Would the grandparent's consent be appropriate if the girl lives with him or her?

Clearly, we might agree or disagree with the conclusion depending on the meaning of parental consent; thus the phrase is an important ambiguity.

The second reason includes another important ambiguity—emotional side effects. Although the writer cites two examples of such effects, our willingness to see this reason as strongly supporting the conclusion will depend on our sense of the frequency, severity, and duration of such side effects.

## What Are the Value Conflicts and Assumptions?

The essay presents an interesting study in value conflicts. To appreciate these value conflicts, you must first uncover a value assumption necessary for the issue to be stated as it is. Before debating parental consent requirements for abortions, one first must be in favor of allowing abortions at all. Individuals who defend abortions are generally referred to as Pro-Choice, referring to the right of the individual to choose whether to have an abortion. Therefore, the author of the passage values the right of the individual to make choices on some level.

However, the individual right to choose conflicts with another underlying value: collective responsibility. The entire argument for parental consent requirements rests on the notion that the adult community has a collective responsibility to curb certain rights of minors. Thus, a value preference for collective responsibility over individual rights clearly influences the writer's choice of reasons and conclusion.

Another value priority can be detected by linking the first and third reasons to the conclusion. Openness and honesty are favored over privacy and autonomy. Asking a parent's permission is being open and honest about one's possible actions. Being open and honest, however, conflicts with a daughter's right to keep certain matters in her life private and to make her own decisions about what happens to her body.

## What Are the Descriptive Assumptions?

For the first, third, and fifth reasons to be true and thus supportive of the conclusion it is necessary to assume that parents will act rationally and in the best interests of their child. This descriptive assumption is questionable. It is quite possible that many parents will get very upset when informed of their daughter's pregnancy, and that there will be a negative impact both on family communication and on the decision-making process. Implicit in the passage is a view of parents as profound, wise, and reasonable. If we believe that this is not typically the case, then we are likely to question the truth of these reasons.

A second significant descriptive assumption underlies the author's claim in the first reason that extending rights to minors "weakens" the communication link between parents and children. By using the term "weakens" the author is assuming that good communication between parents and teenagers who become pregnant currently exists. It is generally acknowledged, however, that parents have a difficult time communicating with adolescent children.

Many minors feel isolated from their parents and would be uncomfortable discussing matters as personal as sexual activity or abortion. It is possible that changing the law might in fact undermine communication and also cause delays in decision making that might be dangerous to the daughter's health. Thus, this questionable assumption makes us question the truth of the reason. A related assumption links the supporting reason to the reason—the idea that the parent is the best person for a pregnant teenager to consult with. Other adults, such as a school counselor or family friend may be more helpful because of being less emotionally involved.

Another descriptive assumption important to the argument is related to the fifth reason. The truth of this reason depends on the assumption that a teen who has an abortion without her parents' consent will not disclose her decision after the procedure. Because having an abortion is such a private decision, the daughter may very well want to wait until after it is over before telling her parents, in which case they can then be alert for possible side effects. If we believe that most daughters reveal their abortions to parents soon after the abortion, then we will doubt the truth of this reason.

## Are There Any Fallacies in the Reasoning?

Several fallacies seriously damage the argument. First, the author diverts our attention from the real issues by using emotional language. Phrases like "rights gone amuck," "impulsive decision," and "lives are destroyed," for example, pull from the reader a negative emotional association to the present law. Also, phrases like "communication link" and "fostering communication" tend to be positive buzz words that create a positive association to the author's position.

The author diverts our attention again when she criticizes Planned Parenthood. She commits an Ad hominem fallacy by attacking the organization rather than its ideas. Planned Parenthood may be biased against parental consent laws, but it also may have good reasons to reject them. The author would have done the reader a favor by focusing on Planned Parenthood's reasons rather than on the issue of financial impact. Both of these tactics divert our attention from the larger issue and from specific, relevant reasons, such as advantages and disadvantages of parental consent laws.

A form of the Begging the Question fallacy occurs in relation to the second reason. The statements in the second paragraph "Would you want your daughter to make an impulsive decision about such an important matter?" and "This law needs to be changed before more teenagers' lives are destroyed" both assume ideas that need to be proven. Evidence has not yet been presented to prove that such decisions are impulsive and that lives are being destroyed.

In addition, the last two arguments are reasoning fallacies. First, the next to last reason commits the Ad populum fallacy by appealing to majority opinion. It makes the erroneous assumption linking the reason to the conclusion that if the majority of the people like something, it must be the right thing. Second, the citing of the support of religious organizations in the final reason is a Questionable Appeal to Authority. We need to ask of such appeals, what are the reasons and evidence for the position?

## How Good Is the Evidence?

First, we ask the question, is there *any* evidence for the claims? There is. Then, we should ask, what *kinds* of evidence does the author provide? The author cites three research studies, two analogies, and an appeal to authority as evidence. A close look at the evidence reveals a lack of *good* evidence.

The bully analogy in the second paragraph is offered as evidence that a minor needs a parent to curb his or her impulsive reactions. Relevant similarities exist between a young child being bullied and a girl deciding whether to have an abortion, such as the desirability of not acting impulsively, and the fact that in both cases, a mistake may lead to dire consequences. The differences, however, question the value of the analogy as evidence. One relevant difference is the age and maturity of the child; older children are typically more mature than younger children. A second major difference is the expected reaction of the parent to the concern. Parents are much more likely to act with strong emotions and moral judgments in the case of potential abortion than in the case of bullying. A third difference is the role of privacy. Contemplating aborting one's fetus is a much more private act than contemplating how to respond to a bully.

A second analogy is used to support reason 4, where it is argued that parental consent is required whenever minors undergo medical procedures— even in the case of getting ears pierced. A relevant similarity is that abortion indeed is a medical procedure. This analogy, however, is subject to the same issues raised by the first analogy—expected parental reactions, and the privacy of the act of carrying a fetus.

The fifth reason points to a survey of gynecologists as evidence that the chance a girl will experience side effects from an abortion is extremely high. This evidence is weak, however, because information about the survey is lacking, leaving important questions unanswered. How many gynecologists were surveyed? Was the sample nationwide, statewide, or local? Was it random? Also, the number of years the respondents have been practicing, and the frequency of different problems, are important, but not included. Without a more detailed description of the survey, it cannot be counted as helpful evidence.

Similar flaws occur in the survey cited in the concluding paragraph. Again, no reference is given to the sample or its breadth. Consider, for example, the possible difference in opinions from a sample of 25-year olds from a liberal state like California and 50-year-olds from a more conservative state like Texas.

## Are There Rival Causes?

Support for the fifth reason is based on a research study that found an association between having an abortion and experiencing depression, implying that abortion was the cause of the depression. But correlation does not prove causation! Rival causes can explain the relationship. For example, individuals who are prone to depression may be more likely to get pregnant and consider an abortion. Level of self-esteem may influence both one's tendency to get pregnant and one's tendency to get depressed, which could cause the association found. Also, dependency on others might influence proneness to pregnancy and proneness to depression.

## Are the Statistics Deceptive?

Some of the statistics deceive us by proving one thing while concluding another. For example, the author of the passage describes the frightening physical and emotional risks associated with abortions to encourage our support for parental consent laws. The statistic that 91 percent of gynecologists had treated patients with complications from legal abortions, however, proves only that most gynecologists have encountered such patients. It certainly does *not* prove that 91 percent of patients have such complications! In fact, the statistic tells us nothing about the likelihood of a complication, given an abortion.

Also, the statistic that 60 percent of women who have post-abortion trauma have suicidal thoughts (cited in the ninth paragraph) is obviously meant to illustrate the grave danger a girl who has an abortion faces. But this statistic proves only that someone with post-abortion trauma is likely to have suicidal thoughts, not that a minor who has had an abortion is likely to have suicidal thoughts. Important missing information is the number of minors having abortions who experience post-traumatic stress syndrome. Perhaps it's only 1 in 1,000.

## What Significant Information Is Omitted?

Because this argument, like nearly all arguments, has incomplete reasoning, the amount of information omitted is vast. To sort through the passage's unanswered questions, you should focus on the most significant of the omitted information.

First, we should ask whether there are relevant pro or con arguments missing. For example, would the author's listing of the arguments of Planned Parenthood lead to a different reaction to the author's reasoning?

Another significant piece of missing information is the evidence to support the author's assumption that minors are unable to handle with sufficient rationality a complicated situation like an abortion. While it might be possible to prove that rationality and judgment are significantly impaired during adolescence or that adolescents have various rational levels of cognition at each stage in their lives, no evidence is given to support or even suggest this idea. The author hopes you will simply equate age with maturity level.

Also, the author fails to consider the potential negative effects of adopting parental consent laws. One such effect of mandatory parental consent laws is the danger they pose to a girl's health. She may postpone seeking her parent's permission for an abortion out of embarrassment or fear of rejection. The longer into the pregnancy she waits to have an abortion, the more dangerous the procedure becomes. Therefore, these laws may delay girls who are inevitably going to have an abortion from undergoing the procedure as early as possible. Another possible negative effect is an increase in the number of "back-room" abortions, giving birth alone, and abandoning of babies, as adolescents wanting abortions search for ways to avoid complying with the law.

Specific information about the frequency and severity of physical and emotional effects of abortions would be helpful in the fifth reason. Also, interviews of minors in states that have and do not have parental consent laws might suggest hypotheses about the impact of not having to notify parents on long-term adjustment following abortion.

Another potential negative effect is more long-term. The implementation of these laws might open the floodgates for more infringement on the rights of minors. The argument is a classic one: if rights can be curbed in one instance, then why not this or that instance? The commonality of the argument should not, however, dissuade us from considering its validity. If the reasoning for parental consent laws is found acceptable and similar reasoning is applied to other issues, such as a minor's right to choose which parent he or she lives with after a divorce, then it is very probable that the reasoning will be accepted again. Before becoming a proponent for this or any argument, you should carefully consider the potential long-term effects of the action.

## What Reasonable Conclusions Are Possible?

Let's first list the reasons that we were least able to criticize—recognizing that all of the reasoning has some flaws. Next we will identify alternative conclusions consistent with these reasons.

1.  Minors are too impulsive and emotional to make sound decisions about abortion.
2.  Parental knowledge of an abortion will reduce the impact of physical and emotional side effects.

Remember that we are looking for conclusions other than the one provided by the author that are reasonable given the most compelling reasons.

One alternative conclusion that is consistent with both strong reasons is for society to make it easier for minors to discuss their situation, both before and after the abortion, with someone other than the parents, such as school counselors, ministers, or clinics. Another plausible conclusion would be to promote more programs to facilitate communication between parents and adolescents. Such an effort might increase the likelihood of minors voluntarily consulting with their parents and making their decisions in a less emotional way.

Another possible conclusion is to educate parents to be alert to signs of depression and other emotional reactions, perhaps through television and magazines.

If it could be demonstrated that older minors are significantly more mature than younger ones, then another possible alternative conclusion that is reasonable is that parental consent for an abortion should be mandatory in certain situations, such as when the girl seeking the abortion is younger than 14.

Our critical discussion responds to only some of the facets of the controversy over parental consent for abortions by minors. You may focus on other parts of the argument. Ultimately, if you care about this issue, you must decide which of the inferences to support. Critical thinking can take you only so far. The final step is yours.

You can feel relatively confident after following our question checklist that you have asked the right questions about the arguments and that you are well prepared to form a reasoned opinion of your own about the quality of the author's reasoning. To reach your own decision on this issue, we recommend that you seek out more relevant information and choose the reasons and values that are most consistent with what you know and what you care about.

# FINAL WORD

Critical thinking is a tool. It does something for you. In serving this function for you, critical thinking can perform well or not so well. We want to end the book by urging you to get optimal use of the attitudes and skills of critical thinking that you have worked so hard to develop.

## The Tone of Your Critical Thinking

As a critical thinker you have the capability to come across like an annoying warrior, constantly watching for ways to slay those who stray from careful reasoning. But learning is in important ways a social activity. We need one another for development; we need one another to share conversation and debate. None of us is so gifted that we can stand alone in the face of the complexities we encounter.

Hence, critical thinkers need to think about what they are giving off when they use their critical thinking. When you use your critical thinking, you are sending some kind of message to others about what critical thinking means to you. This message will be especially effective when it combines the wonder and excitement of the child with the skeptical nature of our best scientists, all moderated by the humility of a monk. Your critical thinking then is on display as a pathway to better conclusions. You seek those conclusions not to elevate yourself above those who have other conclusions, but to move us all forward toward some better understanding of who we are.

Criticism is always a tricky business. In many families and schools, disagreement is identified with meanness. In these settings, the preferred social role is smiling agreement with whatever reasoning is announced. As a critical thinker, you must consider the stark sound of your critical questions in such a context and work self-consciously to make certain that your critical thinking is seen in its best light.

Your best strategy is to present yourself as someone who, like the person who made the argument in the first place, is stumbling around, but always watchful for better conclusions. Whoever finds the better conclusion first is not relevant; what *is* important is the search for better conclusions. If you give signals to those trying to persuade you that you are their partner in a discovery process intended to enrich you both, they may see your critical questions as a tool that is indispensable to both of you.

## Strategies for Effective Critical Thinking

How can you give others the sense that your critical thinking is a friendly tool, one that can improve the lives of the listener *and* the speaker, the reader *and* the writer? Like other critical thinkers, we are always struggling with this question.

Let us conclude this book with a few of the techniques we try to use.

1. Be certain to demonstrate that you really want to grasp what is being said. Ask questions that indicate your willingness to grasp and accept new conclusions.

2. Restate what you heard or read and ask whether your understanding of the argument is consistent with what was written or spoken.

3. Voice your critical questions as if you are curious. Nothing is more deadly to the effective use of critical thinking than an attitude of "aha, I caught you making an error."

4. Request additional reasons that might enable the person to make a stronger argument than the one originally provided.

5. Work hard to keep the conversation going. If critical thinking is deployed like a bomb, thinking on that topic is halted.

6. Ask the other person for permission to allow you to explore any weaknesses in the reasoning. The idea with this strategy is to encourage the other person to examine the argument with you.

7. Convey the impression that you and the other person are collaborators, working toward the same objective—improved conclusions.

We are always eager to hear from any of you who have developed your own strategies for making critical thinking all it can be.

# Index

Jm7084-G

3